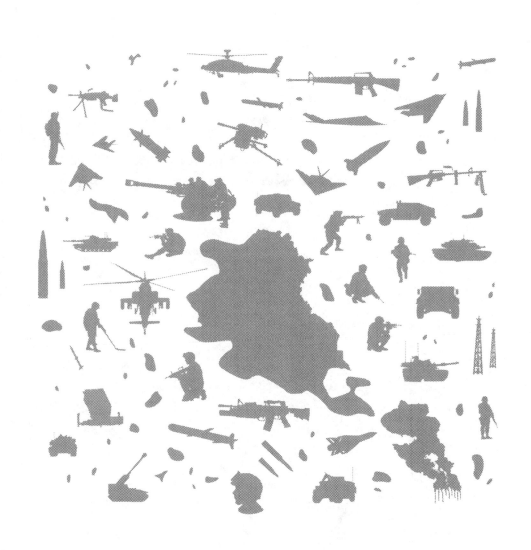

SEMIOTEXT(E) FOREIGN AGENTS SERIES

Published by Semiotext(e)
PO Box 629, South Pasadena, CA 91031
www.semiotexte.com

The Index was prepared by Andrew Lopez.

Special thanks to Nicholas Zurko, Annie O'Malley, Gilda Lavalle, Etienne Li, Mark Polizzotti, Brian O'Keeffe, Olivier Jacquemond, and Manon Plante.

Cover Illustration by Marc Alary
Back Cover Photography by Sylvère Lotringer
Design by Hedi El Kholti

ISBN-13: 978-1-58435-059-0
Distributed by The MIT Press, Cambridge, Mass. and London, England

PURE
WAR

TWENTY-FIVE YEARS LATER

Paul Virilio / Sylvère Lotringer

Translated by Mark Polizzotti
Postscript 1997 translated by Brian O'Keeffe
Postscript 2007 translated by Philip Beitchman

\<e\>

Contents

Paul Virilio

Impure War

introduction to the new edition

The arm race of "Pure War" has exhausted not only the USSR,
which imploded, but also classical "Great War," in favor of
Terror and the terrorist imbalance that we are now experiencing.
Nuclear Proliferation has been unleashed again, taking a turn
towards Fractalization. War is dead, but Terror has replaced it.

Therefore:

After the classical and political "Great War," we now have the
Asymmetrical and Trans-political War of groupuscules, groups,
and other "paramilitaries." The aims of the Anti-City Strategy
shifted from the Balance of Terror to Hyper-Terrorism (2001).
The external "Theater of Operations" is no more: Metro-political
Concentration has won out over Territorial Geostrategy.
Geopolitics has faded in favor of Metropolitics. The Principle
of Indetermination now reigns. Is Globalization Total War?

With *Pure War*, deterrence was military. One practiced reciprocal
deterrence for the sake of the balance of terror. Twenty-five years
later, we're forced to admit that things have changed: the arms race

not only exhausted the USSR, which imploded, but also ended traditional war—political war à la Clausewitz, with its prolongation of war by other means; and all for what? The winners have been terror and the terrorist disequilibrium we've got today, along with a bonus of nuclear proliferation; from which you have this geo-strategic delirium, a madness that effectively arises from globalization. It's being embodied as well by the American global anti-missile cover, an umbrella George W. Bush offered to shelter everyone under. Vladimir Putin's response, in my opinion, was quite extraordinary—it hasn't been noticed enough. He made Bush an offer to install the radar of this global protection…in Russia, in Azerbaijan. It's crystal clear that after the Great War, which was classical and political, we are dealing now with asymmetrical and *trans-political* war. The first time I used this word was in Berlin, some thirty-five years ago. I was in the company of Jean Baudrillard at the time, and I ventured the idea that we were in danger of drifting toward transpolitics. Well, here we are.

When you've called a war asymmetrical and transpolitical, it means that there's a total imbalance between national armies, inter-national armies, world-war armies, and militias of all sorts that practice asymmetrical war. These could be little groups, neighbor-hood or city gangs, or "paramilitaries," as they're called; Mafioso of all types, without mentioning Al Qaeda terrorists, or others. This is what happened in Africa, with countries that have fallen apart; and it's happening right now in Latin America, in Colombia, for example, where the national army is powerless against the prolifer-ation of gangs, mafias, paramilitaries, or guerrillas. In my opinion all of this is contrary to the concept of Pure War.

Today we need to think rather in terms of *Impure War*—I'm not sure it's being called that, surely not—but really the whole question of deterrence has changed in nature. Deterrence is no longer aimed only at the military sector, but essentially at the civilian population; from which we get The Patriot Act, Guantanamo. We can cite similar phenomena in other countries; and, of course, the terrorist disequilibrium. The deterrence of Impure War aims at resisting this disequilibrium; however, reestablishing a balance has become impossible with the proliferation of asymmetrical enemies. There is, in my opinion, an enormous threat to democracy *in every single country*; not only in totalitarian countries, of the East, South, North, or elsewhere, but also in democratic countries, in Europe as well as The United States. With this civilian deterrence—The Patriot Act is a sign, but there are others, for instance certain laws are being considered in Europe governing immigration, etc.—the situation is far more uncertain since we're now resisting disequilibrium. This is called *reestablishing order*, and reestablishing order in civil society means opening the gates to chaos, an absolute threat to democracy of any kind, representative, direct, or participative, as it's called now; and it's clear what this delirium amounts to—a displacement of the *anti-city strategy*.

Let me remind you that the anti-city strategy began with the Second World War, with the bombardments of Guernica, Oradour, Rotterdam, Berlin, Dresden, Hiroshima, Nagasaki. The anti-city strategy was one of the strategies invented during the Second World War. It established the balance of terror, since nuclear missiles, East and West, were targeted on cities. Today, what we're witnessing is a displacement of this anti-city strategy: from the balance of terror to hyper-terrorism. It's especially interesting because hyper-terrorism only knows one battlefield: the city. Whether Madrid, New York, or London, the battlefield is the city. Why? That's where you find a maximum of population and a maximum of damage can be done with a minimum of weaponry, of whatever kind. No need for panzers, giant aircraft carriers, super submarines, and the like. Asymmetrical war, the terrorist disequilibrium has erased the theatre of external operations (battlefields used to be called "theatres of external operations")—in favor of metropolitan concentrations. The battlefield has clearly become the city, the field of the city of men and women. Urban concentration has won out over territorial geostrategy, over front lines, ramparts, Maginot Lines, Atlantic Walls, etc.

For a recent example of the failure of classical war, we need think, not only, of course, of Iraq, but also of the war in Lebanon. The failure of Tsahal in Lebanon is truly extraordinary. The Tsahal is one of the great armies of the Middle East, one of the best equipped, motivated, and supported, yet this army was "trashed," so to speak, in an asymmetrical war against the Hezbollah. Someone called it, furthermore, "a failed war," a stunning nomenclature. Before, wars were won and were lost, now there are failed wars and successful ones; that we're calling defeat *failure* and victory *success* is truly astounding. In my opinion this war revealed the weakness, the uncertainty principle of a normal army, with its tanks, missiles, superbombers, up against a makeshift force. I remember an extraordinary little caricature in a French newspaper; I really should have cut it out: it depicted the Tsahal tanks stopped in the middle of a city in ruins and a sign with a city map, with an arrow indicating "You are here." The tank commander had stepped down to see where he was. I found that an extraordinary illustration of the madness of the day, I'd call it, of a powerful army, flush with its victory in the Six Day War. The Six Day War was still classical war. It still was geopolitics.

Geopolitics meant battlefields, Verdun, Stalingrad, the Normandy Landings. Today geopolitics is fading in favor of what I've called *metropolitics*, insofar as it concerns the city—or rather the metropolis, since London, Madrid, and New York are quasi capitals, not to mention Paris, where attacks against the Eiffel Tower were brewing. After the crisis of geopolitics in favor of terrorist metropolitics, it's now the turn of *geostrategy*; and Vladimir Putin's reply to George W. Bush, "Plant your missiles and radar on our side" highlights the uncertainty about the adversary. There's something humorous about his suggestion, but behind this humor, admittedly absurd, also something true. One may wonder who you're defending yourself against. Putting missiles at the countries' borders, as Bush intends to do, amounts to threatening them even if the missiles are aimed elsewhere. Even if they are aimed at threatening countries like Iran and North Korea, it isn't countries anymore that are at war: the true threat is deterritorialized, or rather delocalized. Therefore the failure of Tsahal against Hezbollah exemplifies the error of contemporary force in dealing with hostilities, with a new delocalized enemy, as opposed to the great revolution of classical Clausewitzian war, which led to Pure War, to the threat of destroying the world through nuclear weapons.

We're entering into what physicists are calling the principle of indeterminacy. The uncertainty principle of Heisenberg, related to *Globalitarianism* and Total War. Is Globalitarian war Total War? No, it's beyond . It is something else entirely. Hence Bush's umbrella. I'm tempted to ask: is it local? And I would answer, "Yes." The size of the battlefield, the length of frontlines count for nothing compared to the immediacy of the threat. When someone manages to sneak an atomic bomb into the New York, Paris, or London subway, this doesn't belong to a total, global logic, but to something local; you're aiming at a city, preferably a large one, to create the maximum of havoc. And it can have the same effect as the battlefields of Stalingrad, Verdun, or elsewhere, had. The war that grows out of Globalitarianism produces a change in scale. Globalitarianism brings us back to the smallest common denominator: one individual equals Total War; and when I say one, it could be ten as well... Just look at the World Trade Center, eleven men brought in twenty-eight hundred dead, just about as many as at Pearl Harbor, with its carriers, Japanese torpedo planes, etc. Exactly the same yield. The cost/efficiency ratio was quite amazing!

Here we're confronting some entirely new situations that put classic war in question, along with geostrategy and the very notion of a frontier. So the joke goes: civil rights, or neighbor's might? From now on we're all on top of each other, all in each other's reach, whether through the airwaves or through the destructive capacity a single man or a small group of men can cause. The great divisions of soldiers of yesteryear, the huge military machines, the gigantic aircraft carriers, like the *General De Gaulle* or the *Eisenhower* are just waiting for a defeat, not from one camp to another, but the defeat of political war. Political war was about a territory and a circumscribed State defending its borders, or else it is civil war. Nowadays there's a Tower of Babel kind of confusion between terrorist civil war—a war against civilians since it's more civilians that are killed, not so much the military, even if the Pentagon was attacked as well—and international war. The two wars are confused, "confounded," I'd say; to the point that I even said to Baudrillard at the time of the World Trade Center attack: "This is the start of the International Civil War." Until now we've had national civil wars: The Spanish Civil War, the Paris Commune, but today this will be our first worldwide civil war.

This is what we're up against with when we raise the question of Pure War. Pure War is still around, it's still possible to press the button and send out missiles—Korea can do it, Iran can do it, and so can others; but in reality the real displacement of strategy is in this fusion between hyper-terrorist civil war and international war, to the point that they're indistinguishable. The dwindling of the Nation-State within great international federations, European development, the NAFTA pact between North and South America (a kind of common market), etc.—means that political, territorial war, linked to a national territory, has ceased to be viable. We are now confronted with a question of the greatest importance, at once political and transpolitical. A huge question mark is rising on the horizon of History.

PURE WAR

1

The Space of War

The City and Politics □ Fortress Europa □ Military Space □ Bunker Archeology □ The Origin of the City □ War and Mercantilism □ "Tumults" □ Logistics □ Urban Sedentariness Commerce and Flux □ Geostrategy, City-States, Nation-States □ Chronopolitics □ The City of Dead Time □ War Culture □ Total War □ The Technical Surprise: War Economy □ Against Sociology

Sylvère Lotringer: *You are one of few French thinkers to have abandoned the language of philosophy or sociology in favor of the war discourse. What leads an architect to study the "archeology" of the bunker? How is it that an urbanist should become interested in the violence of speed, and denounce the death-machine lurking behind the technological adventure? What pushes you to track down the horizon of war in every area of contemporary life?*

Paul Virilio: I am first of all an urbanist. But the relation to the city, for me, is immediately a relation to politics. Furthermore, urbanist and politician, etymologically speaking, are the same thing. Involvement in a political ideology has obscured the fact that politics is first and foremost the *polis*.

And is the city primarily war? How did you come to put war at the center of your concerns?

I'm someone who became interested in war through personal history. As a child I suffered the war; the destruction of the city of Nantes when I was ten was a traumatic event for me. My earliest studies were of military architecture in the Second World War. For ten years I looked for elements of the "European Fortress," and that's how I became aware of the space of war, of the spatial dimension of Total War.

Is there a space of war?

The military space is something people don't talk about too often. You find it in Clausewitz, but it hasn't really been taken up since. People speak of the history of war, of battlefields, of deaths in the family, but no one speaks of the military space as the constitution of a space having its own characteristics. My work is located within this concept. I suddenly understood that war was a space in the geometrical sense, and even more than geometrical: crossing Europe from North to South, from the shelters of the German cities to the Siegfried Line, passing by the Maginot Line and the Atlantic Wall, makes you realize the breadth of Total War. By the same token you touch on the mythic dimension of a war spreading not only throughout Europe, but all over the world. The objects, bunkers, blockhouses, anti-aircraft shelters, submarine bases, etc. are kinds of reference points or landmarks to the totalitarian nature of war in space and myth.

Architecture is always set up as a monument to social thought. The blockhouse is thus crystallized military thought, a city of concrete set up in the space of war. Your Bunker Archeology[1] *explores Total War in its mythic dimensions; but it's also an inquiry into the formation of the city and the future of city planning.*

The city has existed for a long time. It is there to bear witness to the human species' extraordinary capacities for concentration.

How did this concentration come about?

There are two great schools of thought on urban planning: for one, the origins of the crystallization of the city, of urban sedentariness is mercantilism; for the other—the minor one, with Philip Toynbee— it's war, commerce only coming afterward. Obviously I find myself in the minority, which claims that the city is the result of war, at least of preparation for war.

Are you saying the city is not the result of war proper?

Of course there were millions of casualties from the Neolithic Age until the war of the City-State, but these casualties are what the Ancients called "tumults"; they are devastation, things which do not yet have the status of war. Moreover, I agree with Pierre Clastres[2] in saying that it was the "tumult" of the tribes, or if you prefer, the guerrillas, that prevented the coming of the State. When the State was constituted, it developed war as an organization, as territorial economy, as economy of capitalization, of technology. All of this is what will allow for the fortified city and war with projectiles (I am thinking of catapults and all those extraordinary contraptions which, at the time, were the equivalent of our modern cannons).

The general phenomenon is not the economy; it's war.

Let's call it logistics. Logistics is the beginning of the economy of war, which will then become simply economy, to the point of replacing political economy.

What counts in the constitution of the city, then, is not battle, but its preparation.

In ancient warfare, defense was not speeding up but slowing down. The preparation for war was the wall, the rampart, the fortress. And it was the fortress as permanent fortification that settled the city into permanence. Urban sedentariness is thus linked to the durability of the obstacle. Whether it's the rampart of the *oppidum*—of the spontaneously-fortified village in the south of Italy—or that of the ancient city, the surrounding wall is linked to the organization of war as the organization of a space.

Commerce is not linked to sedentariness; it is its result.

The first marketplace was the beach. The Phoenicians pass by in boats (same thing for caravans), they leave an object on the beach, and later they come back to see if anyone has taken it, if anyone has put something else in its place. That's what commerce is: "The caravan passes." This still exists: someone puts a jug of milk on the side of the road and takes off; later he comes back to pick up the money. If there is no money, the jug of milk isn't brought back.

Commerce doesn't need a city.

Commerce comes after the arrival of war in a place, the state of siege, the organization of a *glacis* around an inhabited area, etc. It doesn't need the city—the city in the sense of sedentariness, the mineralization of a building. Mercantilism is even the opposite of sedentariness: it's the stop-over, the rest between two flows.

Your work as an urban planner then, led you to become interested in strategy, or more precisely in geostrategy. And yet you write, in L'insécurité du territoire *[Territorial Insecurity],[3] that contemporary territory is no longer a matter of geostrategy.*

The question has simply shifted. Ancient societies populated space. They gathered at trading posts, then in cities, then in capitals. The City-State was a relative concentration uniting the villages. This concentration repeated itself on a larger scale in the Nation-State and in the creation of the capital, which is the city of cities. It was then a matter, and it's still very often the case, of parceling out geographical space, or organizing the population of a territory. It was geopolitics.

So what political space are we in today?

Today we're in chronopolitics. Geography is the measuring of space. Now, since the vectors of the post-Second World War period, geography has been transformed. We have entered into another analysis of space which is linked to space-time. What we call *azimuthal equidistant projection* is the geography of time. Geography of the day by speed, and no longer a geography of the meteorological day. Already now, when you come back to Paris from Los Angeles or New York at certain times of the year, you can see, through the window, passing over the pole, the setting sun and the rising sun. You have dawn and dusk in a single window. These stereoscopic images show quite well the beyond of the geographical city and the advent of human concentration in travel-time. This city of the beyond is the City of Dead Time.

The urbanist is the man whose art made the city appear; the acceleration of speed is now making it disappear. No doubt an urbanist's sensibility was needed to make the city reappear outside of itself, in excessive forms, in the orbit of war.

This comes from my relation to politics, my relation to death. Let's not forget that in ancient societies, a captured city was an exterminated one, razed, massacred. War was the death of the city, in its stones as in its flesh. My relation to the war-machine has always had a kind of mythic dimension.

Have your theses met with any kind of echo from the military?

I am read seriously by the French military. I have met General Buis and Admiral Sanguinetti, as well as the director of the Hautes Ètudes de Defense Nationale, Xavier Sallentin, who criticized me sharply.

Is there now, in France, any communication between civilians and the military?

In Anglo-Saxon countries, war culture is available to everybody. In London or Berlin you can find practically any book devoted to the military question, including the most recent. In France, war culture doesn't exist, it's censored. The military question is not part of university studies, probably because France is a country in which politics and the military have always been very close.

Does this closeness breed distrust?

It wasn't so long ago that generals held the power in France. And more of that might be in store. I put myself in that position because here it is entirely censored. No one talks about it, no one has anything to say about it, unless to point out that Colonel Bigeard made an ass of himself. That in itself is fine. But to speak of the military as one would speak of philosophy, sociology, or the economy, oh no.

Is the discourse of war better suited to deal with present conflicts than political discourse?

The distinction between military intelligence and political intelligence is becoming outmoded. This is something few have noticed. It goes back to the end of the First World War which was, let's not forget, the first Total War—not the Second. At that moment Georges Clemenceau made a key statement: "War is too serious to be confided to the military." That was the last political statement by a French politician (there have been others elsewhere in Europe). It is there, in the economy of war, in the involvement of the economy of European societies in war, that the coherence of the political discourse dissolves and that strategy definitely replaces this type of reasoning.

How do you explain this transformation?

Political society of the nineteenth century was formed in schools, in colleges, with teachers, in a very historical, historicistic manner. The model for teaching in France and Europe was the Jesuits. Thus it was a neo-military education. Up until the First World War, we had politicians, civilians educated in the knowledge of war by the Ancients, by the memory of Napoleon. These politicians really were civilians, because they had had a military education. They were able to make the generals dance to their tune. They had the same power of analysis in the facts of war as the officers did. Now, after the First World War a split occurred, which was furthermore considered positive, between the political discourse and the increasingly technical discourse of war. Let's not forget that World War I was the first truly technical war in Europe (in the United States, of course, there had been the Civil War, which was already a Total War). After several months of trench warfare—that is, of position warfare, since the armies could no longer move—they realized that their current war production, the traditional production foreseen during peacetime, could no longer meet the demands of military consumption (in the number of shells fired, of bombs, planes, etc.). And this on both sides, for Germany as well as for the Allies. This was the "technical surprise," as it was called, of World War I. So all of a sudden, there was a tragic revision of wartime economy. They could no longer simply say that on one side there was the arsenal which produced a few shells, and on the other, civilian consumption and the budget. No, they noticed that they needed a special economy, a wartime economy. This wartime economy was a formidable discovery, which in reality announced and inaugurated the military-industrial complex.

It's the end of civilian society.

It's the end of the economic rationale of "political economy."

The civilian becomes the military.

The notion of "civilian" becomes perverted. It loses its meaning. People often tell me: "You reason in a political way, like the Ancients." It's true. I don't believe in sociology. It's a mask. Sociology was invented in order to forget politics. For me, all that is social, sociology, doesn't interest me. I prefer politics and war. So when I say that there is a perversion, I mean in fact that the situation is no longer very clear between the civil and the military because of the total involvement of the economy in war—already beginning in peacetime.

It a Copernican revolution in the relations of strategy to politics.

Absolutely.

2

The Time of War

Three Imaginary Orders □ The Tendency and Myths □ Eisen-
hower □ Tactics and Strategy □ The Nuclear Bomb □ Logistics □
The A-national Military Class □ Ultimate Weapons □ Military
Intelligence? □ The Disappearing Military □ War and Science □
The Technical Enigma

*You reject sociological analysis, but in its place you put a mythologi-
cal model, the structure of the three "functions' (sacred, military,
and economic) established by Georges Dumézil*[4]* through the collective
representations of Indo-European society. Indo-European tripartition is a mythical projection more than an historical reality. What
allows us to accord it an analytical capacity greater than that of contemporary sociology?*

Myths have an analytical capacity that cannot be denied. By com-
parison sociology seems a surface effect. What interests me is
tendency. As Churchill wrote: "In ancient warfare, the episodes
were more important than the tendencies; in modern warfare, the
tendencies are more important than the episodes." Myth is tendency.
The three functions thus seem to me analyzers of the knowledge

of war, of political knowledge, achieving infinitely more than all the successive sociological macro- or micro-developments. Of course a tendency is not a reality, it's a statistical vision. The myth as analyzer and as tendency is itself also of a statistical order.

I have the feeling that the Indo-European tripartition, like many other structures, has become visible to us by the very fact that it is in the process of disappearing. Without going so far as to envision, as Jean Baudrillard[5] does, an inversion of all the poles and their eventual implosions, we must recognize that it has become difficult to maintain the distinction between the civilian and the military.

There is no need to maintain it. But Dumézil's analysis, the analysis of European history through the three orders—through the imaginary of feudalism, as Duby[6] would say (he scarcely quotes Dumézil, which is rather striking)—allows us to understand the tendential development of Western society. We find priests, warriors, and peasants in contemporary society with overlays that cause the priest to be no longer simply a preacher, and the warrior no longer simply a soldier, but also a military engineer, or the engineer of advanced techniques. The peasant is also the proletarian, but the proletarian is also the professor, insofar as teaching has been discredited, etc.

Dumézil, like Duby, speaks of castes. Does a military caste still exist? Can we understand the contemporary military phenomenon as the mythic projection of a caste analyzed in Indo-European societies?

That is still a pertinent mechanism for the distribution of tendencies. This doesn't mean that the mythic institution of a caste (caste of warriors or priests) still has meaning today. Its reality has of course become more diffuse, and that is why I speak of a military class. But the caste has taught us more about Indo-European society, or Western society to be simpler, than sociological analysis. I don't have much use for sociological analysis. Moreover, it doesn't seem very well-founded, whereas we could find a connection between the myths of Indo-European tripartition and those of contemporary sociology. I'm thinking of Roland Barthes: sociology as mythology.

According to Roland Barthes, the function of myth is to immobilize the world. You do just the opposite: you use mythology to get a hold on current transformations and to set thought in motion. But we had stopped at the point where the creation of war economy perverted the distinction between civilian and military institutions. Did this tendency increase after World War I?

For the Second World War, war economy was prepared long in advance, very seriously, especially in England. Furthermore, England was to serve as a model of wartime production for a man like Albert Speer. He was very clearly inspired by it, particularly by the air force—that is, by spearhead weapons. What allowed England to win—aside from its naval power, which was old—was the ability to develop a super-sophisticated air force in a very short time. The U.S. then entered the scene with Eisenhower who was, don't forget, a specialist in war economy and the preparation of the means of waging war. And there we have the development of a completely unique and extraordinary machine, which in fact eventually became a State within the State.

This State within the State is less national than it seems. In fact, it has more to do with the logistical machinery of other nations than with its own civilian society. Aren't we already seeing here the building-up of what you call an a-national military model?

Absolutely. Eisenhower was, to my mind, the first to represent a kind of confusion between the states. We know of his rivalry with Montgomery. A traditionalist like Montgomery sensed quite well that his role as Colonel Blimp, as old vet, as old militarist was becoming outmoded because of the logic of production and the logistic tendency of American economic power-economic in the sense of a war economy. Why Eisenhower? It's not that he was a great war leader, but that he was a man of the war discourse. He was the only one to use the new concept, which was logistics.

What preceded this concept?

There are three phases of military knowledge. The tactical phase is the first, since it goes back to hunting societies. *Tactics* is the art of the hunt. *Strategy* appears along with politics—politics in the sense of *polis*, the Greek city—the strategist who governs the city, the organization of a theater of operations with ramparts and the whole military-political system of the traditional city. Of course, tactics continue, but now there is, let's say, a supremacy granted to strategy over tactics which furthermore explains the development of military elites, particularly the horsemen, just as much the Roman horsemen as the medieval knights who followed. Around the 1870's, the *war economy* suddenly appears. We notice it in English, then in French budgets with the development of naval artillery and the battleship. All of this culminates, as we have seen, in the technical surprise of the First World War. Finally we have the great surprise, no longer technical but scientific, a surprise of another kind: the advent of the nuclear bomb. It's no longer a quantitative problem that surprises the military staff, and thus the states; now it's a qualitative problem: the ultimate weapon. Logistics takes over.

What is meant exactly, as this point, by "logistics"?

Logistics is a word that people don't understand. It is a term that comes from the Prix de Rome, *logiste*, "competitor," and which was used by Henri Jomini, Clausewitz's theoretical adversary. In his treatise on war, Jomini has a large chapter which is the first to appear on logistics, and it's an inquiry: What is that thing that makes it no longer enough to have war-intelligence—I put my battalions on the left, I charge on the right, I surprise them at dawn, etc.? How is it that the means become so important? Jomini realizes that it's the Napoleonic wars, thus already mass wars, technical wars, with artillery and the Chappe telegraph which appeared at that time. Between the already sophisticated artillery and the telegraph, you have a situation—a primitive one, granted, but which nonetheless represents rather well what will later develop in the audio-visual field, in long range artillery, and finally in missiles. Logistics occurs at the time of the Napoleonic wars because these wars pulled millions of men onto the roads, and, along with them problems of subsistence. But subsistence isn't everything: logistics is not only food, it's also munitions and transportation. As Abel Ferry said, "The munitions problem runs parallel to the transportation problem." The trucks bringing ammunition and the flying shells bringing death are coupled in a system of vectors, of production, transportation, execution. There we have a whole flow chart which is logistics itself. To understand what this a-national logistical revolution—Eisenhower's—is, there's a statement by the Pentagon from around 1945–50 which is extraordinary: "Logistics is the procedure following which a nation's potential is transferred to its armed forces, in times of peace as in times of war."

The logistical revolution means, in short, that the civilian finds himself discriminated against in favor of a kind of crystallization of the scientific and the military. But under these conditions, can we still say where the military begins, and where it ends?

When I say "the military," I don't mean a military caste. On the contrary, what occurs with the triumph of logistics is a class, something more diffused, less definable. An a-national military class, insofar as war today is nuclear or is not at all. When we speak of conventional warfare and nuclear warfare, or of limited war, unlimited war, Total War, we are playing with words. It's obvious that the advent of the ultimate weapon has completely modified the question of war. Moreover, deterrence is there to prove it. We must not be mistaken: there is a war phenomenon which is linked to the ultimate weapon, to the possibility of using the ultimate weapon, and also to its logistical preparation.

If the military class is no longer a caste, but rather something more diffuse, less identifiable, more insinuating, what could it mean to be anti-militaristic today? A moment ago you answered: I am not an anti-militarist, I'm worse. But wouldn't this ethic of the worst be a way of making up for the caste's failings, a way of recapturing at the last minute a class which is "nowhere to be found"? By aiming for the worst, don't you help substantiate the idea that, although it's submerged, disseminated, elusive and obsessive, although it confused with civilian society and therefore with ourselves (where does technology begin and where does it end?), that somewhere there is still an enemy against which a just battle can be fought—and thanks to which we can consider ourselves on the side of the just?

The anti-militarist is a racist. He is someone who attacks man. One is anti-militarist the way one is anti-priest. One sees a cassock and one spits on it; one sees a uniform, same thing…. I find that ridiculous. I am against military intelligence, I am not against men of war. Why? Because I've known them, they're the same! There's no difference between a union member in a brawl and some poor slob of a sergeant, or a low-ranking officer (we'll leave the high-ranking officers aside, there is still the matter of administrative responsibilities). They are dominated, whether they know it or not, by the war-machine. So my opposition to war is an opposition to the essence of war in technology, in society, in the philosophy of technology, etc…. My opposition is not an opposition to men: I easily mix with generals and admirals, and I have absolutely no racist reflex. Naturally, if they tried any form of putsch, I would be the first to oppose. But they are no more responsible for the apocalyptic nature of war than the civilians. The proof is that they are disappearing, too! They're disappearing in the technology and automation of the war-machine. Look at the war of the Falkland Islands, it's very revelatory. Take the captain of the "Sheffield" and the pilot of the "Super Ètendard." The pilot answers to the slogan of the Exocet missiles: "Fire and forget." Push the button and get out of there. You go home, you've seen nothing. You fired forty, sixty kilometers away from your target, you don't care, the missile does it all. On the other side there's the "Sheffield" captain who says: "In this war, everything happens in a few seconds, we have no time to react." You see two military men in uniform; one an Argentine pilot, the other a veteran of the Home Fleet, who say: "The missiles go by themselves. We are finished...." I am not against the military as people are against priests, I'm against the intelligence of war that eludes politics.

But aren't we all caught in the military enclosure? Don't all of us in some way participate in its enterprise?

All of us are already civilian soldiers, without knowing it. And some of us know it. The great stroke of luck for the military class's terrorism is that no one recognizes it. People don't recognize the militarized part of their identity, of their consciousness.

Is what you call the "military class" proper represented only by the military, or does this also include all those who continue to build up its power?

Let's say that it includes all who contribute, directly, or indirectly to organizing this Pure War. Of course it's the strategists who work at this ideology of the unacceptable, the engineers of armament. And it's just as much the multinationals which invest in an apoca-lyptic—officially apocalyptic—perspective, on the economic level. We are on the verge of 1929. The crash could happen tomorrow. It could have happened yesterday. So what I call the "military class" includes all those who reason within this technological logic.

It's what gives this "techno-logic" a kind of unity.

The so-called "technocrats" are very simply the military class. They are the ones who consider rationality only in terms of its efficiency, whatever the horizon. The negative horizon's apocalyptic dimension doesn't strike them. It's not their problem. In this sense they're not priests. When I talk with a general or an admiral, I'm always struck by his lack of knowledge about nuclear destruction, his ignorance of the experience of this destruction. It doesn't interest him. We notice that the doctrine of use—in other words knowledge at work in effectiveness, utilization—has been completely squeezed out in favor of a doctrine of production: they make tools so that they exist for a war in its pure form, without worrying about what happens when you use them. Which brings about the aberration of the Falklands war, in which British ships are sunk by machines perfected either by the British themselves or by their friends (the French). That's what the military class is, that kind of unbridled intelligence which gets its absence of limits from technology, from science. The war-machine is not only explosives, it's also communications, vectorization. It's essentially the speed of delivery. When Esso tells the French national train company: "We'll stop delivering containers, materials, gasoline, oil, refining products, unless you guarantee us trains with 4000-ton capacity running at an average of 100 km/hr"; when Esso threatens to make do with trucks, it's already war. Pure War, not the kind which is declared.

For a long time now, we've been hearing about permanent revolution. Now we can say that Pure War is permanent war.

It's war operating in the sciences. It's everything that is already perverting the field of knowledge from one end to the other: everything that is aligning the different branches of knowledge in a perspective of the end.

Is the answer along the lines of Ivan Illich's conviviality, in other words the restriction of the role of technology to its individual dimension?

Science and technology came from man's questions about Nature. It was from this revealed knowledge about the riddle of Nature that technology was produced. Since then—for about a century now—the riddle of science and technology has tended by its development to replace the riddle of Nature.

Technology is our new Nature?

It is our Nature. And there are no scientists or technicians to answer this riddle. More than that, there aren't any because they refuse; because the scientists and engineers, claiming to know, don't allow anyone to inquire into the nature of technology. And so the riddle of technology becomes more fearsome, or at least as fearsome, as the riddle of Nature.

Thus your work, which is epistemological, or rather "epistemo-technical."

3

Technology and Trans-Politics

Heidegger □ War and Technology □ Deterrence, Peace and Total War □ End of Politics □ State Terrorism □ Transpolitics and Duration □ Instantaneous Destruction □ Politicizing Speed

"Epistemo-technical" is a very good word. The question of technology, as Heidegger said, is to question. Heidegger began to do it, we have to recognize, and perhaps he did it precisely because he knew the question of technology through futurism, in other words, fascism.

Any examination of technology immediately gives rise to misunderstandings, and your work is no exception. Your writings have been interpreted as a defense of technology, and your warnings seen as a denial of the fascination you unquestionably feel toward it—and toward war. From the outset you have put yourself in the position of military officers, the better to question them. But as we find in your work neither a recognizable political stance nor traditional ideological references, this has created around it quite a lot of ambiguities, some of them pretty funny. Before meeting with you, I had heard that you were a captain in the French army having gone lock, stock, and barrel over to the camp of philosophy.

riddle of the accident. I'll explain. In classic Aristotelian philosophy, substance is necessary and the accident is relative and contingent. At the moment, there's an inversion: the accident is becoming necessary and substance relative and contingent. Every technology produces, provokes, programs a specific accident. For example: when they invented the railroad, what did they invent? An object that allowed you to go fast, which allowed you to progress—a vision à la Jules Verne, positivism, evolutionism. But at the same time they invented the railway catastrophe. The invention of the boat was the invention of shipwrecks. The invention of the steam engine and the locomotive was the invention of derailments. The invention of the highway was the invention of three hundred cars colliding in five minutes. The invention of the airplane was the invention of the plane crash. I believe that from now on, if we wish to continue with technology (and I don't think there will be a neolithic regression), we must think about both the substance and the accident—substance being both the object and its accident. The negative side of technology and speed was censored. The technicians, by becoming technocrats, tended to positivize the object and say, "I'm hiding it; I'm not showing it." There's a lot to be said about the *obscenity* of technology. That's where you find technophilia.

Was the violence of speed censored? Is that the reason for the fascination it inspires and the repulsion people feel toward it?

In technical terms, speed is a transfer of energy. We can summarize this in two words: "stability-movement" and "movement-of-movement." Stability: I don't move, I am still. Movement: I am in motion. I speed up: movement-of-movement. The passage from "movement" to "movement-of-movement" is a transfer of energy, what we also call an "accident of transfer." Once you start thinking in terms of energy, the problem of violence is immediately present. Currently, there's a debate over the La Villette Museum of Science and Technology. I want to make a provocation-proposal requesting that next to the Hall of Machines they put a Hall of Accidents. Every technology, every science should choose its specific accident, and reveal it as a product—not in a moralistic, protectionist way (safety first), but rather as a product to be "epistemo-technically" questioned. At the end of the nineteenth century, museums exhibited machines; at the end of the twentieth century, I think we must grant the formative dimension of the accident its rightful place in a new museum. They ought to exhibit—I don't know how yet— train derailments, pollution, collapsing buildings, etc. I believe that the accident is to the social sciences what sin is to human nature. It's a certain relation to death, that is, the revelation of the identity of the object.

So all is not negative in the technology of speed. Speed and that accident, that interruption which is the fall, have something to teach us on the nature of our bodies or the functioning of our consciousness.

Exactly. That's what I say in *The Aesthetics of Disappearance.*[7] The book's main idea is the social and political role of stopping. The break taken for sleep has been worked on a lot by psychoanalysis, but I have absolutely no confidence in psychoanalysis. In fact, all interruptions interest me, from the smallest to the largest, which is death. Death is an interruption of knowledge. All interruptions are. And it's because there is an interruption of knowledge that a time proper to it is constituted. The rhythm of the alternation of consciousness and unconsciousness is "pic-nolepsy," the picnoleptic interruption (from the Greek *picnos*, "frequent"), which helps us exist in a duration which is our own, of which we are conscious. All interruptions structure this consciousness and idealize it.

All things considered, the concept of death as accident, as interruption of knowledge, is relatively recent. It is in fact contemporary with the constitution of knowledge about man. The more they individualized man in the heart of our culture, the more they made his death the great cut-off, an insurmountable interruption.

Epilepsy is little death and picnolepsy, tiny death. What is living, present, conscious, here, is only so because there's an infinity of little deaths, little accidents, little breaks, little cuts in the sound track, as William Burroughs would say, in the sound track and the visual track of what's lived. And I think that's very interesting for the analysis of the social, the city, politics. Our vision is that of a montage, a montage of temporalities which are the product not only of the powers that be, but of the technologies that organize time. It's obvious that interruption plays more on temporality than on space. It was no accident that religious thought instituted all sorts of prohibitions, holidays—the Sabbath, etc …. They regulated time, they were aware of the necessity of stopping for there to be a religious politics. Why? Because religious politics was defined with respect to death, to the great interruption, to the "last judgement," as they say in the Scriptures ("Apocalypse"). It's a positive fact, because it gives technology a new status. Technology doesn't give us anything more, it interrupts us differently. To be interrupted in a car is different from being interrupted while walking.

The connection of the driving body with the locomotive body is a connection to a different type of speed-change. Interruption is a change of speed. The strike, for example—I mean the general strike—was a formidable invention, much more so than the barricades of the peasant revolt, because it spread to a whole duration. It was less an interruption of space (as with the barricade) than of duration. The strike was a barricade in time.

This aesthetic of interruption which structures contemporary consciousness is, in fact, a cinematics. For the cinema, art of the continuous, paradoxically gets all its energy from interruption.

The cinema shows us what our consciousness is. Our consciousness is an effect of montage. There is no continuous consciousness, there are only compositions of consciousness. And these compositions are voluntary and involuntary: I decide to take a nap, I belong to a system that forces me to rest on Saturday, or Sunday, or Ramadan. These are conscious interruptions, the result of a will. And then there are unconscious interruptions like sleep, picnolepsy. Even if I don't want to, I fall asleep. It's a collage. There is only collage, cutting, and splicing. This explains fairly well what Jean-François Lyotard calls the disappearance of the great narratives. Classless society, social justice—no one believes in them any more. We're in the age of micro-narratives, the art of the fragment. It's not by chance that one of the greatest books published in France is the one by Mandelbrot on *Fractal Objects* (the geometry of fragmentation). Dimension doesn't have to be whole, it can be expressed in fractions. For many natural objects (the coast of Brittany, for example), dimensional unity is an abusive simplification. We see that there has been a displacement of unity (the notion of the unity of continuity), onto the notion of fragment, of disorder. And there we have a reversal. The fragment recovers its autonomy, its identity, on the level of immediate consciousness, as Bergson would say. History is on the level of the great narrative. I only believe in the collage: it's transhistorical.

Do you think that State terrorism, State delinquency, is the fragmentation of general war as we have known it in this century?

The great narrative of Total War has crumbled in favor of a fragmented war which doesn't speak its name, an intestinal war in the biological sense.

It's a kind of puzzle that no longer has any unity. War happens everywhere, but we no longer have the means of recognizing it.

This recognition of the fragmentation of historical reality is the dawn (we are still being metaphorical) of an identity, a world-wide consciousness. Just as we could say: "My lived time is mine and I'm conscious of it because there are interruptions," I would say: "We are going toward the pure State because there is an infinite fragmentation of interstate conflicts." In other words, we're going toward the common consciousness that we are all earthlings, identical—with all the fearsome and monstrous things that presupposes.

Parallel to the fragmentation of history in a multitude of micro-narratives, we see a kind of mythological epic on the horizon, the epic of nuclear death, a planetary and global vision founded on the imminence of our civilization's collapse.

It's the mega-interruption. Individual death founded all of religious, mystical and magic thought. From the recognition of the death of tribes, of the group, they then arrived at the idea that civilizations, too, are mortal. With nuclear weapons, the species is now recognizing the possibility of its own death. Nuclear holocaust reintroduces the question of God—no longer on the scale of the individual or of a chosen race, but of the species. It reinterprets man's role.

And yet it helps restore a unity to humanity.

Its only truth is the negative horizon.

The end of time, or the end of temporality, as the ultimate advent of humanity.

It's interesting to privilege interruption on the level of chrono-politics, as opposed to geopolitics. Interruption in space was the ramparts, rules, chastity belts. Now interruption in the body is replaced by interruption in time. We plug into everyone's intimate duration. Subliminal effects mean just that.

At the same time it's the death of intimacy. All the reflection of these last years on an exploded, "schizophrenic" model of subjectivity corresponds to the great aesthetic of the collage. The ego is not continuous, it's made up of a series of little deaths and partial identities which don't come back together; or which only manage to come back together by paying the price of anxiety and repression.

But from the moment you say that the essential thing is to contemplate death and examine the interruption, you go much further.

Schizophrenia stumbles over the question of death, in the sense that materialism gives it; disappearance means it's the end, nothing's left. Whereas death is a mysterious interruption, like picnolepsy, sleep. To say that there's nothing left after death is crazy. To my mind, *that's* where idealism lies. If we want to give interruption all its value, we must include death in it. Of course we don't wake up from it, but in picnolepsy you don't wake up either, since you don't even realize you were asleep.

It's also by interruptions that writing is worked on well. Nietzsche wrote in aphorisms, which are interruptions of thought. I particularly admire the suggestive, rather than explanatory, side of your own approach.

I don't believe in explanations. I believe in suggestion, in the obvious quality of the implicit. Being an urbanist and architect, I am too used to constructing clear systems, machines that work well. I don't believe it's writing's job to do the same thing. I don't like two-and-two-is-four-type writing. That's why, finally, I respect Michel Foucault more than I like him.

When everything has been said, nothing's left. Your approach, on the contrary, is resolutely telescopic. As soon as you hook something, you let it go, you jump aside instead of saturating the area you had invested. It's a whole politics of writing. It's not an organized discourse of war, even less a discourse on war; it's a discourse at war. Writing in a state of emergency.

I work in staircases—some people have realized this. I begin a sentence, I work out an idea, and when I consider it suggestive enough, I jump a step to another idea without bothering with the development. Developments are the episodes. I try to reach the tendency. Tendency is the change of level.

This is somewhat new in the area of theoretical writing.

Yes, absolutely. In *L'Esthétique de la disparition*, I had the revelation of the importance of interruption, of accident, of things that are stopped as *productive*. It's entirely different from what Gilles Deleuze does in *Mille Plateaux*.[8] He progresses by snatches, whereas I handle breaks and absences. The fact of stopping and saying, "let's go somewhere else" is very important for me. I relate it to things like the strike. The essential thing in a strike is that you use absence.

Each landing is the stopping of theoretical work. So that something else can happen.

So that something else can happen and a space can appear. Claims to go all the way around a question are absurd. You can't shape it. One should not try to get all around a question. There are only successive perspectives.

Speed and Politics *is a rapid book.*

It's a rapid book, but it's a key book. It's not the amount of pages that counts; I never write long things. My great reference point is not Clausewitz, but Sun Tsu. His *Art of War* is only 120 pages long. *Speed and Politics* is an important little book because it was the first to raise the question of speed. It's an introduction to a totally new world which has never been shown before. Not many writers have touched on speed. There is of course Paul Morand, some Kerouac, but that's literature. For a more political vision of speed, there's Marinetti and the Italian futurists, and then Marshall McLuhan who took a step in that direction; that's all. *Speed and Politics* is not so important for what it says as for the question it raises.

Speed and Politics *is a theoretical accident.*

Yes, which is why it doesn't last very long.

What seduced me from the beginning is precisely that a book on speed should be so rapid. We've gotten too used to seeing "the end of the book" proclaimed in books that are themselves interminable. Your work is not voluminous because it is itself "vehicular." Actually, that's the title of the last chapter of L'insécurité du Territoire, *of which* Speed and Politics *is in some way the theoretical complement.*

The last chapters of my books are always important because in the final account I don't believe in writing several books. You could publish them in an enormous dictionary in which everything would come chronologically. In "Vehicular," I began to realize certain things. I realized that the question of war was summed up in the question of speed, of its organization and production, in short of everything that surrounded it. So after *L'insécurité du Territoire*, I put out a text which was less rich in developments, but richer from the theoretical point of view—which was precisely *Speed and Politics*. All of my books form a whole. I'm now about to put out a book which develops and completes many aspects of *Speed and Politics*. It's called *La stratégie de l'au-dela* [The Strategy of the Beyond], subtitled "Dromoscopies," and this led me to *L'Esthétique de la disparition*, which bears the effects of my interest in the missing, in disappearances. All of this is echoed.

What is the strategic position of Speed and Politics *in your works?*

It's an essay that can serve as a tool with which to analyze ancient societies as well as contemporary ones, and perhaps even the future, since it allowed me to analyze several recent events in the audio-visual field along the lines of the development of the automobile and the cinema.

You subtitled Speed and Politics *"Essay on Dromology." How would you define this new science, or this new relation of science to thought?*

"Dromology" comes from *dromos*, race. Thus it's the logic of the race. For me it was the entry into the world of speed-equivalent and wealth-equivalent.

5

Speed and the Military

Speed and Wealth □ The Dromocratic Revolution □ The Ultimate Weapon □ Going to Extremes □ The End of Politics □
Technical War and Holy War □ Non violence

*Let's come back to the idea, which is so central to your work, that
wealth has obscured speed in the founding of politics. Is this a recent
phenomenon, or is it an ancient one which has only recently passed
over the "critical threshold"?*

Speed is the unknown side of politics, and has been since the
beginning; this is nothing new. The wealth aspect in politics was
spotlighted a long time ago. Now, it was a mistake—which I'm
modestly trying to correct—to forget that wealth is an aspect of
speed. One usually says that power is tied in with wealth. In my
opinion, it's tied in first and foremost with speed; wealth comes
afterward. Of course it's true that power needs means, that it
acquires these means either by hoarding, exploitation, or both, but
people forget the dromological dimension of power: its ability to
inveigle, whether by taxes, conquest, etc. Every society is founded on
a relation of speed. Every society is dromocratic. If you take Athenian

society, you'll notice that at the top there's the hierarch, in other words the one who can charter a trireme. Then there's the horse-man—the one who can charter a horse, to use naval language. After that, there's the hoplite, who can get ready for war, "arm himself"— in the odd sense that the word armament has both a naval and a martial connotation—with his spears and his shield as a vector of combat. And finally, there's the free man and the slave who only have the possibilities of hiring themselves out or being enlisted as energy in the war-machine—the rowers. In this system (which also existed in Rome with the cavalry), he who has the speed has the power. And he has the power because he is able to acquire the means, money. The Roman horsemen were the bankers of Roman society. The one who goes the fastest possesses the ability to collect taxes, the ability to conquer, and, through that, to inherit the right of exploiting society.

We are now reaching the point at which material development is a direct function of military development.

And only that. This brings me back to some ancient but clear-cut examples. We have two sides of the regulation of speed and wealth. Up until the nineteenth century, society was founded on the brake. Means of furthering speed were very scant. You had ships, but sailing ships evolved very little between Antiquity and Napoleon's time; the horse even less; and of course there were carrier pigeons. The only machine to use speed with any sophistication was the optical telegraph, then the electric telegraph. In general, up until the nine-teenth century, there was no production of speed. They could produce brakes by means of ramparts, the law, rules, interdictions, etc. They could brake using all kinds of obstacles. (It's not by chance that ancient society was one of successive obstacles on the level of people, of morals, of territorial definition—whether it was the city walls, taxes, the fortified systems of the Nation-State: all of them were so many brakes.) Then, suddenly, there's the great revolution that others have called the Industrial Revolution or the Transportation Revolution. I call it a dromocratic revolution because what was invented was not only, as has been said, the possibility of multiplying similar objects (which to my mind is a completely limited vision), but especially a means of fabricating speed with the steam engine, then the combustion engine. And so they can pass from the age of brakes to the age of the accelerator. In other words, power will be invested in acceleration itself. We know that the army has always been the place where pure speed is used, whether it be in the cavalry— the best horses, of course, were army horses—the artillery, etc. Still today, the army uses the most pertinent speeds—whether it be in missiles or planes. Take the example of the uproar around the American SST. It wasn't built because the Americans were very worried at the idea of building a civilian supersonic jet that would go faster than military jets. It's very clear that the hierarchy of speed is equivalent to the hierarchy of wealth. The two are coupled. And there, indeed, the state of emergency, the age of intensiveness, is linked to the primacy of speed, and not only on the scale of a more-or-less effective cavalry or naval weapon.

So the primacy of speed is simultaneously the primacy of the military.

Absolutely. Dromocracy takes its rightful place, but this time on the scale of a world society in which the military classes are in some ways the equivalent of what the feudal lords were in ancient society. There is no political power that can regulate the multinationals or the armed forces, which have greater and greater autonomy. There is no power superior to theirs. Therefore, either we wait for the coming of a hypothetical universal State, with I don't know what Primate at its head, or else we finally understand that what is at the center is no longer a monarch by divine right, an absolute monarch, but an absolute weapon. The center is no longer occupied by a political power, but by a capacity for absolute destruction.

On the one hand we have the decline of the State, which is the end of history, and on the other we have a state of emergency, which sanctions the absolute power of the instant.

History as the extensiveness of time—of time that lasts, is portioned out, organized, developed—is disappearing in favor of the instant, as if the end of history were the end of duration in favor of instantaneousness, and of course, of ubiquity.

But this instantaneousness is also nuclear power.

This instantaneousness is linked to the center, and the center is nuclear power. The invention of the scientific surprise—the great scientific surprise of 1945, the ultimate weapon—moves to the center of political debate; it dissolves political debate.

It's the intrusion into political debate, where everything is negotiable, of another dimension—something irreducible, irreversible. One can negotiate around nuclear power but not over the ultimate weapon.

The gravest danger of this ultimate weapon, the nuclear weapon, is that it exists and that by its very presence it disintegrates any debate on societal evolution.

The gravest danger is not nuclear firepower, but what you call "nuclear faith," faith in nuclear power And yet, paradoxically, what corresponds to the end of classical war is a kind of exacerbation of local conflicts; what corresponds to the end of the Nation-States are all kinds of resurgencies in pro-war sentiment, archaisms, terrorism, etc.—on all levels, furthermore, including State terrorism, as with the Falklands. Is it just a temporary phenomenon about to vanish, or an inversion related to the disappearance of territorialities?

It's a definite inversion. I believe we're heading toward universality. The universe-city; the universal city. The fact that today we have Yalta agreements and East-West confrontations, that we have NATO, SEATO, the Warsaw Pact, etc.—to my mind, all of this has been outmoded by a kind of universal State, a State in its pure form which is the result of Pure War, that is, of the intensity of the means of destruction. Capitalist and Communist ideologies are themselves being superseded by this vision of the world. The problem today is that the true enemy is less external than internal: our own weaponry, our own scientific might which in fact promotes the end of our own society.

The possibility of instant destruction is superseding strategies of deterrence. We're now entering into a new phase which could be characterized by "going to extremes." It could lead us to Apocalypse (absolute destruction), unless it rapidly brings about the negotiation of a new Yalta. Is this "going to extremes" an unheard-of phenomenon?

"Going to extremes" is one of Clausewitz's concepts. It designates the relation he draws between war and politics. Clausewitz is a man of political war. Going to extremes is the tendency of war to go beyond all limits. We said a moment ago that war exists in its preparation: setting up the fortified city and organizing: battalions, discipline, strategy, etc. But within this process of preparation and organization, there is a tendency toward escape. An infernal tendency—heading toward an extreme where no one will control anything. There, Clausewitz says something fundamental: "Politics prevents complete release." It's because war is political that there is not complete release. If war weren't political, this release would reach total destruction.

"Going to extremes" becomes a reality because politics is losing its role as arbiter of conflicts. The end of politics, then, doesn't mean a reduction of ideological antagonism, but eventually the end of our civilization. We have defined a—shall we say—positive aspect of death: death reunifies, nuclear death gives us back a mythology on the universal level, it promotes a new humanism founded on destruction. There is a second aspect, entirely negative this time, which has to do with this mythology holding an insurmountable threat over our civilization, giving rise to a reign of terror in the name of death which is at hand, but perhaps will never arrive. Consequently, it risks causing a wave of demobilization: if nothing can really prevent a nuclear holocaust, any form of resistance becomes useless; even fragmentary life collapses before this threat.

That might come from the fact that there are no priests of nuclear death other than military men. Death only exists as a foundation of religion because there are intercessors—I almost said intellectuals—mediators of the death question on the individual level: those who come to hold your hand as you die, those who make a sign of the cross over the condemned man, those who give absolution, etc.

Now, for the death of the species, there are no priests. The only mediation is by the military, and it's obvious that the military man is a false priest because the question of death doesn't interest him. He's an executioner, not a priest. A new inquisitor. And as he is the inquisitor of all thought—not only within civilian society, but within science itself—war is now infiltrating the social sciences.

It certainly seems that with General Sharon, we saw an escape from politics that went to extremes.

Absolutely. The war in Lebanon indeed went to an extreme that ties it in with the Holy War. Personally, I'm totally against Holy Wars, even against the ideology of a "just" war, because if Israel and Islam furthered the Holy War, they would be making the jump from political war. They can accept complete release because they are religious. They're religious in a tnumphalist way: they use the fact that they don't believe in death, the fact of their awareness of the non-ending of life, to go beyond politics. And as a Christian I do the opposite; I say, "No, it's the abomination of desolation." On the contrary, we have to turn back. In the name of a belief that death doesn't exist, that there is an afterlife, we must not only forbid Holy Wars—wars of complete release—we must also refute the justness, the justice of war. The theology of the "just war" must be abolished by the Pope at a time when the Holy War is starting up again in Lebanon, when it's spreading between Iran and Iraq. Because the Holy War, given existing technology, is a complete release.

Not only is it the end of politics, it's also the end of any ethics.

Before nuclear power, the "just war" had meaning. It had meaning in politics. Technological war, on the other hand, is complete release. It's already the beyond. We're there as soon as we accept the idea of a holy or "just war" with nuclear power. We're already in the apocalypse, which is annihilation. The apocalypse is no longer the revelation of the soul's immortality, but the extermination of all bodies, all species, all of Nature, everything! Today, the Holy War is on the horizon of our history.

Our history started in the Middle East, and it's in danger of ending there. Religious fanaticism and technological absolutism are an explosive mix.

To my mind, the politics of a Begin or a Khomeini, and there are others, is an opening onto nuclear war. That's how nuclear war could happen. I would even say: "That's how someone who doesn't believe in nuclear war could, accidentally or not, unleash nuclear war." To me, this is sheer madness—the warrior of Holy War and the technician of nuclear war.

Pure War and Holy War are the same thing for you.

The Islamic Holy War was the equivalent of Pure War in people's minds. It was a complete faith which caused thousands of men to go to their deaths convinced of their immortality. I can't judge the Holy War of the Crusades. But now, even the "just war" doesn't exist.

Do you think we can still use the war-machine against the State-machine? Is it possible to fight the State with war (urban guerrilla tactics, in particular)?

I don't think so at all. The national States already have too many means in their possession. National States are kernels of States in their pure form, conglomerated bits of pure State. One cannot use violence against what is already violence, one can only reinforce it, take it to extremes—in other words, to the State's maximum power. Just look at Italy, for example. Today, the only recourse is nonviolence.

6

Deterrence and Freedom

of Movement

Zero Growth □ Deterrence and Dromological Power □ Generalizing Deterrence □ Nuclear Monarchy □ Polar Inertia □ A Society in Transit □ The Capital of the End of Time

We haven't taken the path of nonviolence. On the contrary, it's in violence—in the nuclear threat—that we've confided the task of ensuring peace.

The belief in salvation—in peace—by means of the ultimate weapon is an idolatry; it's obscurantism, there's no doubt about it. It works like a military-scientific cult, which no one dreams of challenging. This has brought the Holy War back into light. In the face of the "Pure War" of weapons, of this ideal of an ultimate weapon able to ensure the survival of the species, etc., a forgotten debate has been revived: that of the Holy War, which is the counterpart of Pure War.

But this belief in salvation through the ultimate weapon is what we called deterrence.

Nuclear faith means believing in deterrence. It means believing that the fact that the weapon doesn't explode is a good thing. What I have just said is exactly the opposite. The weapon's serious danger is not that it could explode tomorrow, that there could be five million deaths, but that for thirty years it has been destroying society (and causing endo-colonization).

Does the development of a war economy entail the disappearance of civilian society?

It's obvious that the complete release of political war is the complete investment of political economy in war economy. The development of technology is Pure War. Logistical necessities, confrontation of blocs result in a conflict on the technological level. Weapons and armor constantly need to be strengthened. Technological development thus leads to economic depletion. The war-machine tends toward societal nondevelopment. We can say that ecological necessities of "zero growth" run parallel with *ecologistical* necessities of zero growth! On one hand it's a matter of not depleting resources, on the other of not developing civilian society because it hinders the development of military society, the means of waging war. The current belief is that there's going to be a conflict between industrial societies and underdeveloped countries, a North-South conflict. But the problem is not underdevelopment. The underdeveloped countries are not developing: we are all becoming underdeveloped.

Deterrence is still a form of persuasion. We appeal to reason to justify the unjustifiable. But behind this screen, we get the impression that something like a final solution on the planetary scale is being set in place.

Deterrence is the emotive phase of dromocratic power. There are various aspects of power, which we can call: moving-power (or power to promote), knowing-power, and finally emoting-power (power to move emotionally). Knowing-power, or "power-knowledge," was developed by "historeticians"—I repeat, historeticians ....

Like Michel Foucault.

Like Michel Foucault. For there to be knowledge, there has to be pro-motion, for knowledge is inquiry. It's the result of a penetration into territory. The knowing-power of the monks exists because there were conquests, because there was pro-motion—setting armies in motion, setting the Crusades in motion, setting populations in motion to go and gather the echo of civilizations, etc.

Does dromocratic power; what you call pro-motion, necessarily precede knowing-power?

Before knowing-power, there is always moving-power, or pro-motion, the last phase being emoting-power. Now, an ideology corresponds to nuclear pro-motion—ballistic speed of missiles, laser beams—which is nuclear faith in deterrence.

We haven't reached the end of ideology so much as the advent of ideology, in its deterrent form.

Deterrence is the last ideology.

But isn't deterrence itself losing its logistical value?

We have entered the second phase of deterrence. All-points deterrence is succeeded by all-weapons deterrence, on all levels of weaponry. Relative deterrence from the means of nuclear strategy becomes a general, generalized deterrence. The generalization of deterrence is the new question that confronts us at the end of this century. The current debate on the development of conventional armaments, on the exponential growth of military budgets in the US, France, or the USSR, is not only interesting on the first level, which led society to nondevelopment. On the ideological level, it conveys above all the idea that deterrence must be generalized. I think that no one has really considered what that could mean: *generalized deterrence*. Moreover, I can't answer completely, except to say that it's suicide. Cultural suicide. That is certain. An obscurantism is pervading all levels of society.

It's perhaps the prelude to the disappearance of our civilization, as other civilizations have suddenly disappeared with no explanation. Deterrence is the last ideological rampart against a kind of global destruction.

That would still be to believe in history. To believe in the idea that there is an afterward, that there will be an extension into the future as there was one into the past. Personally, I believe that the existence of nuclear weapons is deterrent in that we could all disappear. A billion casualties on the face of the earth would not be negligible, but they would have died in vain, for the nuclear weapon still exists, it is there. It even exists in blueprints by students who are practically able to jerry-rig a nuclear bomb in their own kitchens; all you need is some plutonium. It's this very existence that constitutes the drama. How do you "kill" the ultimate weapon? We could say the same thing about what happened in 1789. How do you kill the monarch after a revolution which has done away with monarchy? The dead monarch returns as Emperor. So this less-than-bourgeois revolution was in fact military-bourgeois. It brought about the Empire. The military-industrial complex also came about that way. Today the question would be: How do you kill nuclear monarchy, the weapon present "by divine right" at the center of our society, of our societies? That's the real question.

So how do we get rid of it?

My only answer is that the question of speed is central. Furthermore, I'm not the first to have said it. General Fuller, one of the great historians of military affairs, an Englishman, said that the essential thing in the nuclear age is speed. An interesting statement because, first of all, it's not clear. The problem is not the destructive power of the new weapon—the weapon of Hiroshima—but its speed. And we must recognize that in the age of deterrence, something has not been deterred. If civilian economies have been deterred to the point of tending toward nondevelopment, something has nonetheless continued to be developed, which is speed. It's the speed of these vectors which in 1961 led to the "hot line" between Khrushchev and Kennedy, and which leads today to quasi-instantaneous decision-making.

In other words, deterrence is still a humanist category because it implies time for reflection.

Right, we no longer have time for reflection. The power of speed is *that*. Dromocracy is that. Dromocracy is no longer in the hands of men, it's in the hands of computerized instruments, answering machines, etc. Today there is still a reaction-time. It was approximately half an hour in 1961. Andropov and Reagan have no more than several minutes.

Several minutes are all that remain of man.

They're all that remain of man's power. Of course, it all depends on where you fire from. The satellite-weapon can be fired from space, and thus right onto the United States. It's immediately on-site. The nuclear submarines are much more alarming, all they need is to be near American or European territorial waters. They've calculated the delay: it's about fifteen minutes for intercontinental missiles, and two to five minutes for the most efficient submarines or unidentified objects in space. Except that, unfortunately, for the last ten years 80 percent of military research in the Soviet Union and the United States—and in France as well (although less than 80%)—has been devoted to laser weapons. Now, a laser beam moves at the speed of light, in milliseconds. That's nothing at all. It practically means mastering instantaneousness. Which means that by the end of the century, the ultimate weapon will have acquired absolute speed.

Absolute destruction will correspond to absolute speed. At that point, there will be no room left for man.

There will be no more man, there will only be weapons. The real question of monarchy, of nuclear monarchy, is *there*.

What strategies can we adopt to fight this exponential growth of destructive power?

There has been incredible research done into the economy: into the question of production, of wealth in the generic sense (with Adam Smith, Marx, etc.). But we're backward when it comes to the economy of speed. Now this work has to be done. Today, the target is to try to have an understanding of speed. Understand what's been happening for twenty-five years.

This would come down to taking the knowledge of speed away from the military in favor of civilian society.

Right. To try to comprehend—in the sense of inclusion—the effect of speed on the time of societies, and on the space-time of societies. Take the urban crisis in the United States and Europe. Hot summers are no longer simply the hot summers of the 1960's in the US. With the crisis of the urban capitals; it's also the crisis of industrial centers like Liverpool, the London suburbs, Brighton, the Lyons affair in France, etc. Last year there were similar riots in England, and everything seems to indicate that France will see its share of them in the coming years. So what does that mean? There have been many socio- and ethno-analyses (the ghetto, etc.) of this phenomenon. As for myself, I see it a different way, which is that we are in the middle of a process of deurbanization.

The technological race has caused the city to disappear.

The city was the means of mapping out a political space that existed in a given political duration. Now speed—ubiquity, instantaneousness—dissolves the city, or rather displaces it. And displaces it, I would say, in time. We have entered another kind of capital, which corresponds to another kind of population. We no longer populate stationariness (cities as great parking lots for populations), we populate the time spent changing place, travel-time. What we are noticing on the level of urban planning has already been noticed on the level of specific neighborhoods, of individuals, even of being at the mercy of phone calls. There is a kind of destruction caused by saturating immediacy, which is linked to speed. So it seems to me that the danger of nuclear power should be seen less in the perspective of the destruction of populations than of the destruction of societal temporality.

I feel all the more concerned by this destruction, having recently returned from Nepal where, for lack of roads, you can only get around on foot. It's probably the last country in which distances are calculated in days of walking, which furthermore are very elastic. Yet it only takes several hours to get to Nepal by airplane....

We generally distinguish three types of distance. Space-distance is the day of walking, or the kilometer, to simplify; then time-distance, the kilometer/hour; and finally speed-distance, which is the mach. Movement is no longer indexed according to metrics, but to the speed of sound. Thirty years ago, for example, it took twenty-four hours to go from Paris to New York. Now it takes three and a half. By the end of this century, with the hydrogen jet, it will take only half an hour. But at the same time, it still takes over three and a half hours to go from Paris to Corsica. So there is a deregulation of distance which causes time-distances to replace space-distances. Geography is replaced by chronography. The mach-meter of the Concorde replaces the kilometer. There's something very important in that.

We have begun to inhabit time.

For a long time the city existed just where it was. Paris was in Paris and Rome in Rome. There was a territorial and geographical inertia. Now there's an inertia in time, a polar inertia, in the sense that the pole is simultaneously an absolute place (for the metaphor), absolute inertia which is geographically locatable, and also an absolute inertia in the planet's movement. We're heading toward a situation in which every city will be in the same place—in time. There will be a kind of coexistence, and probably not a very peaceful one, between these cities which have kept their distance in space, but which will be telescoped in time. When we can go to the antipodes in a second or a minute, what will remain of the city? What will remain of us? The difference of sedentariness in geographical space will continue, but real life will be led in a polar inertia.

Man will no longer need to move because he won't be at home anywhere.

The proximity of the world will be such that "automobility" will no longer be necessary. This is already happening through the speed of audio-visuals, with tele-conferences and televised debates. When physical mobility catches up with the performances of electronic mobility, we'll find ourselves facing an unheard-of situation of the interchangeability of places. That in fact is the current project. This situation was unthinkable several generations ago; philosophers told us that instantaneousness, ubiquity were unthinkable by their very essence. I myself deny this unthinkableness, precisely because I'm not a philosopher. I put myself on the level of technology. Technology is what allows this ubiquity, and we can now begin to think about it. Proximity, the single interface between all bodies, all places, all points of the world—that's the tendency. And I push this tendency to extremes. It's not science fiction. Science and technology develop the unknown, not knowledge. Science develops what is not rational. That's what fiction is.

But is this fiction developed by science beneficial? Does the ubiquity of technology open new spaces of freedom to man, or rather does it drastically reduce his margin of movement?

One always says that the primary freedom is freedom of movement. True, but not freedom of speed. When you go too fast, you are entirely stripped of yourself, you become totally alienated. There can be a dictatorship of movement.

Is technology, then, not progress so much as alienation?

Since the eighteenth century—since the Age of Enlightenment, to use the well-known terminology—we have believed that technology and reason walked hand-in-hand toward progress, toward a "glorious future," as they say. It went without saying that we would find the solution: to sickness, to poverty, to inequality. We found it, all right, but it was final, not optimal. It was the solution of the world ending in nuclear war, in Total War, in extermination and genocide. Thus, my intention is to say: No more illusions about technology. We do not control what we produce. Knowing how to do it doesn't mean we know what we are doing. Let's try to be a little more modest, and let's try to understand the riddle of what we produce. Inventions, the creations of scientists are riddles which expand the field of the unknown, which widen the unknown, so to speak. And there we have an inversion. This inversion is not pessimistic per se, it's an inversion of principle. We no longer start from a positivistic or negativistic idea, we start from a relativistic idea. The problem is the following: technology is a riddle, so let's work on the riddle and stop working only on technology.

What is the riddle of the city for a technician of urban planning? You say that in the future cities will disappear in the vector of speed. But after all, isn't it to speed that the geographical city itself owes its existence?

The city has always been a box full of speeds, a kind of gearshift. The organization of cities is the streets. What are streets? Rushes. In Greece they don't say a street, they say "a run" (*dromos*). As long as the possibilities of acceleration were negligible and the city defined much more by ramparts than by highways, it was believed that cities didn't organize speed. And yet when you look at Greek urban planning (the city of Miletus for example), colonial planning or that of the Roman camps, you see quite well that the roads are rectilinear. It's an organization of speed to drain the populations as fast as possible toward the city gates, toward the outskirts. A city is not simply a place where one lives, it's above all a crossroads.

Thus acceleration makes the very essence of the city reappear, this essence being to convert the social space into a temporal "clutch lever."

This is why the airport today has become the new city. At Dallas-Fort Worth they serve thirty million passengers a year. At the end of the century there will be one hundred million. People are no longer citizens, they're passengers in transit. They're in circumnavigation. When we know that every day there are over one hundred thousand people in the air, we can consider it a foreshadowing of future society: no longer a society of sedentarization, but one of passage;

no longer a nomad society, in the sense of the great nomadic drifts, but one concentrated in the vector of transportation. The new capital is no longer a spatial capital like New York, Paris, or Moscow, a city located in a specific place, at the intersection of roads, but a city at the intersection of practicabilities of time, in other words, of speed. Perhaps that is the Eternal City now. Not the capital of a region, empire or belief, Rome or Jerusalem, but the Capital of the End of Time.

If the airport has become the new city and its citizens passengers in transit, does anything remain of the city in space? Doesn't it continue elsewhere, in forms of sedentarization which are just as violent and extreme as its polar abolition?

To the extent that the inertia of the city of the future is not the inertia of immobility, but the dictatorship of movement, it is possible that catastrophes will occur which will be serious enough to drive people back to their primary habitats. This is what seems to be happening in South America and in many other regions where, next to fabulous airports, you see shanty towns develop which are infra-urbanisms. They prove on the contrary that absolute movement is falling apart, not only because of the energy crisis, but also because of our inability to set up a true vectorial politics—something like a democratic speed.

The answer to the citizens in transit of the beyond are the squatters of the inner cities. Does the breakdown of movement in polar inertia suggest, in the heart of the future city and not only at its outskirts, the existence of new modes of enclosure?

When a businessman travels from Paris to New York, New York-Paris, Paris-New York, New York-Paris by Concorde, he begins to experience the situation of polar inertia. This new form of sedentariness is the active tendency in technology. Sedentariness in the instant of absolute speed. It's no longer a sedentariness of non-movement, it's the opposite.

It's the sedentariness of transportation.

That's right. The sedentaries of transportation are very simply travelers who buy a plane ticket at Roissy-en-France or Orly—for Roissy or Orly. They go around the world as fast as possible without going anywhere, barely making the necessary refuelling stop, and nothing else. An empty voyage, a voyage without destination, a circular voyage, which puts immediacy to the test. In the last several years we have seen the appearance of many afficionados of this kind of voyage. What is the pleasure in taking the Concorde if it's only to return at the same instant, or in the few hours that follow, to the point of departure? There's a mystery in that, a riddle of displacement that fascinates me. I think it's a form of desire for inertia, desire for ubiquity, instantaneousness—a will to reduce the world to a single place, a single identity.

7

The Colonization of Time

Technological Conquest □ The Empty Circle □ The Dictatorship of Movement □ An Imperial Mythology □ The War of Time □ Howard Hughes □ The Invalids of Time

These afficionados of movement are the new explorers of the chronological imaginary, settlers of the technological continent.

Just as there was a colonial influence of the means of progressing in space, the *conquista*, colonization, and cultural conquest, there is a colonization, a technical conquest of the means of transportation, of the airplane, of television, etc. I believe that those who volunteer for this kind of trip without destination experience a situation of oneness, of identity ultimately without value, with no other value than to be possessed by one alone. I am one with the world. It's the myth of Jules Verne, but a myth which is no longer in eighty days, which is barely in hours, which is already inscribed in a system of seconds. A day, no longer of passing time, but of speed itself. The day which allows us to witness the other side of the world live on television.

It's the speed of light.

Yes. I believe that it's this kind of day which is tested in that empty circle. That extra day—a kind of false day. The false day of speed that the technology of the Concorde today, and more sophisticated technologies tomorrow, will allow us to achieve.

The false day of speed is one that never quite arrives.

Before, you had to leave in order to arrive. Now things arrive before anyone's leaving. We can wonder what we will wait for when we no longer need to wait in order to arrive. The answer: we'll wait for the coming of what remains. These sentences seem paradoxical, but they aren't: the end of departures, generalized arrivals…. That's what the passengers of the empty circle are trying out, what they're already outlining by hurrying to go nowhere. Of course they still leave and come back for the moment, but they're waiting to be able to arrive without leaving.

Speed is not progression or progress, but the involution of the trip, the "eternal detour" of the same. The will to impotence?

Speed allows for progress in space, only progress in space has been identified with progress in time, in history. And that is really an abuse of language. We know very well that progress in space is not necessarily progress in time. The fact of going faster from Paris to New York doesn't make the exchanges any better. It makes them shorter. But the shortest is not necessarily the best. There again it's the same illusory ideology that when the world is reduced to nothing and we have everything at hand, we'll be infinitely happy.

I believe just the opposite—and this has already been proven—that we'll be infinitely unhappy because we will have lost the very place of freedom, which is expanse. All current technologies reduce expanse to nothing. They produce shorter and shorter distances— a shrinking fabric. Now, a territory without temporality is not a territory, but only the illusion of a territory. It is urgent that we become aware of the political repercussions of such a handling of space-time, for they are fearsome. The field of freedom shrinks with speed. And freedom needs a field. When there is no more field, our lives will be like a terminal, a machine with doors that open and close. A labyrinth for laboratory animals. If the parceling out of territory—of territories of time—is envisioned like that, according to a strict regulation and not a chrono-political under-standing, there will be nothing left but absolute control, an immediacy which will be the worst kind of concentration.

Haven't we already witnessed this inversion in the past, with territo-rial conquest?

As Fuller says, every offensive is exhausted by its very success. We saw this with the Wermacht's advance into the Eastern countries. The advance of logistics, stretching supply routes to the maximum, causes the offensive to wear itself out by its own success. To my mind, something of this nature is happening with the exponential development of vectorization. The infinite acceleration of auto-motive means: aviation, missiles, the absolute acceleration of railway transportation, the magnetic train, the hydrogen jet, the space shuttle; all of that absolutely exhausts the absolute offensive.

What do you mean exactly by "absolute offensive"?

Absolute offensive is absolute movement in that it is not politically controlled, it is not reasoned out, it is the fruit of technology and nothing else. Technology infinitely promotes speed, and this promotion is absolute depletion to the extent that it's technological progress that decides, and not a rationale. It's not a philosophy of movement. We pass from freedom of movement to tyranny of movement.

The free traffic of goods and persons, the "laissez faire, laissez passer" attitude that defined the space of freedoms—even if they were liberal freedoms, thus not so free after all: would all that become its opposite if pushed to extremes? Are we now condemned to nomadism, at the very moment that we think we can make displacement the most effective means of subversion?

It was believed that freedom of movement led to infinite freedom. I have shown it's not true: there's a dictatorship of movement beyond a certain limit. That's what I mean by exhausted offensive.

It is inversion, its extenuation.

Exhaustion is polar inertia. To the extent that we are in limited surroundings, the exhaustion of absolute movement is practically upon us. Polar inertia means that in not too many years—several decades at most, but certainly less—the world will be so restricted that we will be one on top of the other in time. In space, we'll still be at considerable distances. But audio-visual and automotive relations will have concentrated us into an inertial confinement—which will be the reduction of the world to nothing. Howard Hughes represented this situation very well. It's the breakdown of absolute movement: inertia in a finite world.

The planet is shrinking, but the universe is expanding. Can we make an abstraction of all that surrounds us?

The moon and the stars are all part of the Western imperialist illusion: "The world is not finite, we have conquered America, tomorrow we'll conquer the moon, etc., etc...." It's absurd. Of course there will be people hopping around the stars. But the question now confronts us in geographical limits. If we don't ask it now at least within the limits of the world, exhaustion will be still more absolute.

In other words, the cosmos is a mythology of inertia.

An imperial mythology! The last form of imperialism is to say that the universe remains to be conquered—after having made of world conquest what we did, in other words the depletion of the Third World, etc....

It's an extension of terrestrial war into interplanetary space.

It's an extension of the nineteenth century: an extension into "space." In the nineteenth century, before relativity, one economized time in space. The fourth dimension came very late. Western expansionist policies economize time; the policy-makers don't realize that in geographical space there's a nongeographical time, which is an inertial limit. When there's less than a minute to decide whether or not to push the panic button, we will have reached a limit, which is of the automation of war. The decision for war or peace will belong to an answering machine! Those are time-limits which weren't taken into account in the nineteenth century.

Imperialist designs on the conquest of the star don't take into account the fact that we are limited in time, enclosed in duration as we are limited in space. Modern war has already moved from space into time. It's already a war of time. Of course it will still happen somewhere, but in this place time is much more important than space. Military space is first and foremost technical space, a space of time, a space of the rapidity of attack and reaction. The nineteenth century didn't take time into account, the twentieth is forced to. And the limits are not in space. The time-limit allowed us is draconian, it's time to realize this. We are not at liberty to travel in time.

You often mention Howard Hughes. Do you think he was the first citizen, as well as the first victim, of this capital of dead time?

Howard Hughes is an extraordinary figure because he dreamed of owning the world, and ended up proving that one can become autistic precisely because one owns it all. Everyone thought Howard Hughes was crazy; to my mind, he went crazy from that very sedentariness. He's a man who lived to the limit of polar inertia. He was the first one to close the empty circle, in the thirties, with his Lockheed Cyclone—note that it wasn't a Mystère or a Phantom, it was a *cyclone*…. He came back to the same spot, New York. Howard Hughes was the Lindbergh of the end of the world, a hero of post-modernism. Afterward he invested enormously in aviation, he set up movie studios. He had a hand in everything that appeared at that time having to do with speed, the airplane, and the cinema. He tried to enjoy his omnipresence in the world. First he lived by having several apartments all over the world, each decorated the same way. Every day he was served the same meal, brought the same paper at the same times, taking into account the differences in time zone. Then that situation became unbearable and he ended up a technological monk in the desert of Las Vegas, without getting out of bed. He spent the last fifteen years of his life shut up in a hotel tower, watching films, always the same ones, especially an old American film on the life of men shut up in "Ice Station Zebra" in the North Pole. He saw it 164 times. I remember this number which shows that for him, inertia had become not only a physical reality (he really was bedridden), but also an object of fascination: he never stopped watching a film that represented exactly that same inertia in a polar city, a city of scientific research, always eating the same dishes, surrounded by the same cars, Chevrolets, as banal as could be. This man had lost the world because he had won it.

Like power, speed must be atoned for. Now, Howard Hughes owed his power to speed. In this, he is doubly exemplary.

What fascinated me about Howard Hughes, more than the man himself, was the fact that he had managed to foreshadow a *mass situation*, the quest for the progress of speed without the knowledge of the engine's exterminating character. Howard Hughes is the metaphor for everything that's now happening in every social situation. He lived inertia and the intensity of supermovement to the death.

The peak of speed is the extermination of space. The end of time is absolute deterritorialization.

Yes, absolute. The tendency is for each place to become rigorously equivalent. And if technological developments continue, we'll have reached this in two or three generations. Just consider the magnetic train project in the United States, the hydrogen jet and even, very simply, the daily efforts of television—it's already polar inertia. Who are these people fascinated by their electronic windows? There we have a phenomenon of inertia and death on the spot which geographical sedentariness represented for the nomads of the steppes, but which is now situated in time. A sedentariness in dead time.

Movement paralyzes. Movement kills motion. Speed pushes us into a paradoxical space in which all the terms are inverted.

Movement is now only a handicap—a double handicap that we know only too well. A motor-handicap: a man in a car piloted by a driver (until such time as cars are completely automatic, which won't take long) is motor-handicapped. In his own way, he is just as bedridden as Howard Hughes. The man sitting before his television watching the soccer championship live from Santiago in Chile is seeing-handicapped. For example, to be—as we are now—sitting in well-stuffed chairs is a postural comfort. Our muscles are relatively relaxed. They aren't being called upon. It's a postural comfort with respect to the body and to physiological materialness. Now, the prostheses of automotive audio-visual movement create a subliminal comfort. Subliminal, meaning beyond consciousness. They allow a kind of visual—thus physical—hallucination, which tends to strip us of our consciousness. Like the "I run for you" of automobile technology, an "I *see* for you" is created. The prosthesis grafts itself onto physical movement: it helps us go faster—on a bicycle, a motorbike, in a car. This ends up multiplying the vivacious being, the metabolical vehicle that I am: I, pedestrian, passer-by. Subliminal comfort multiplies the speed of consciousness—the speed of the vivacity of reflexion. This multiplication can be pleasant in relative acceleration, that is, within the boundaries of my consciousness; but these boundaries are very narrow, and if, as in certain cases of "invasion of privacy," someone should use speed to go beyond this, I am conditioned. This in fact is what is called subliminal advertising and, of course, propaganda directed at entire populations. You see an image of which you are not at all conscious. It imposes itself on you without your being able to detect it, because it goes too fast. The prosthesis is completely alienating.

8

Cinema and Resistance

Italian Autonomy Underground Radio □ Revolutionary Resistance □ The Dissolution of the Avant-Garde □ Speed and Perception □ The Aesthetics of Disappearance □ The Society of Disappearance □ The Suicide State

The Italian Autonomists were the first ones to show me Speed and Politics. *At the time they were confronted with problems of guerrilla warfare which weren't theirs, but which they couldn't ignore, as "terrorist" struggles against the State (by the "Red Brigades") were little by little entailing their own elimination from the Italian political scene. In return, they were turning to technology in an attempt to regain political initiative. Thus they had a certain faith in the positiveness of technology. It's what they called (especially in Bologna) not military intelligence, but "techno-scientific intelligence." Does it bother you that there are misreadings of your thought and that it has been used in a different way in the Italian context, despite everything you're trying to say?*

It bothers me, but it doesn't surprise me much. It bothers me because it has never been the case in France, a country where there hasn't been terrorism in the Italian sense. In fact, I had heard through the grapevine that in Italy they *had* interpreted my work as being pro-technology. I was very surprised at first. That's why I wrote *Popular Defense and Ecological Struggles*, in which I questioned the tactics of the Red Brigades. I know they heard it. I've also published interviews in *Metropoli* to denounce that mistaken interpretation.

As for yourself, you have never believed in the possibility of diverting technology.

No. I'm thinking of people like Lanfranco Pace and Franco Piperno, very involved people; I'm thinking of Nanni Balestrini who is hiding out in France. I told them that the only work to be done was epistemo-technical. The problem is not to use technology but to realize that one is used by it. So it wasn't a matter of using technological instruments, whatever they may be—television, free radio, etc.—but of working on the essence of technology in its relations to politics. And some of them are doing this work.

In a tactical way, then, you are even against the reappropriation of technology by the underground "free radio"?

I think that with the "free radio" as with the rest, technology was used without an understanding of what was being used. When you spend several thousand francs on material for a free radio, you know how to buy, you know how it works, but you don't know what to do while on the air! We see the results in France. It's a kind of infinite cacophony, of airwave saturation. We can't really say that it's free. There again you find limitations—in time.

What did you think of the Italian Autonomist movement? Of course it ended up being crushed by the combined action of the two war-machines. Still, was there anything important in it that survived the event?

Absolutely, and on a number of points. The will to autonomy was the will to get away from cultural and political conformity. I do nothing different: my work is in this direction.

Do you think that autonomy was bound to fail or that it could have won, given the specific conditions in Italy?

Independently of Italy it cannot be condemned, since there's nothing else to be done. I don't believe in revolution, but I do believe in revolutionary resistance. That requires widening the rift, as much as you can, in an inquiry which becomes more and more essential, in a return to our identity as mortal beings—to our statute as occupants of time—and not only to wealth, places, space. All the work of consciousness raising within the Autonomist movement was originally that: science, and nothing else! Mind you: the origin of science is not the elites, it's people who began to wonder about phenomena, just as much on the level of dietary customs as of little rural techniques. There were the greats, Euclid, etc., but today everyone must work at trying to interpret the riddle of technology! I don't believe that scientists will find the solution. It's in every man's autonomy that this reinterpretation of machines, situations, etc. must be performed— under pain of death, because there's no time. That's my position.

Reflection can just as well crystallize around social experiments. What struck me in the Italian situation was the social chemistry effected by the juncture of the collective organization of the "squatters"—founded on "archaic" community practices—and the futuristic impulse of the free radios: the juncture of technological abstraction and politicized sedentarizations. It's this very heterogeneous aspect of the factors active in the Italian situation that constituted a full-fledged techno-political reflection.

There were some very original things—which furthermore haven't been lost—in the Italian experiment. That's why I wasn't a failure. It would have been a failure had they really aimed at changing society: but they knew very well that other things were needed in order to change society, something other than a small movement. When I speak of revolutionary resistance or popular defense, I'm getting to the root of an essential popular scientific invention. I remember the speeches in the Richelieu Amphitheatre of the Sorbonne, before the taking of the Odéon Theatre at the very beginning of May '68. I went in: the place was packed. I heard a guy, probably a Communist, say, "I read on the walls of the Sorbonne: 'Imagination comes to power!' That's not true, it's the working class!" I answered: "So, comrade, you deny the working class imagination." It was pretty clear, one referring to a horde able to take power like a mass of soldiers, and the other (me) referring to the active imagination—the Autonomists. On this level.

But '68 was a kind of poetic metaphor, and Italian Autonomy the attempt to literally implant it in conditions which were always specific.

The Italian Autonomists failed in a Marxist perspective, according to which you have to change your life. I, for one, believe that it is not yet within our reach. The Autonomists invented questions. They found a few answers, but in no case did they find answers able to change their lives. It's not life we have to change, it's death; it's the relation to duration; which is also the feeble duration of political currents. I published a book by René Lourau on the manifestoes of *The Auto-dissolution of the Avant-Gardes.*[9] There's something there which I completely agree with: only the movements which were able to cease, to stop by themselves before dropping dead, have existed! The Autonomists, if they shut down operations, if they tip their hats saying, "We've done our thing, we're leaving the stage, we can't do any more," show that they're not Stalinists, that they aren't inscribed in history.

In the end, the diaspora of autonomy is still autonomy. The fact that they chose to disperse over the world is a new form of political experimentation on the planetary scale. And we should start gathering the seeds of this experiment, instead of seeing this dispersal as a failure. We should watch how autonomy, confronted with different conditions, can continue to germinate.

Absolutely. The question of action has always been a problem for me because my vision is still of a scientific order. While continuing to work on dromology (*Speed and Politics*), I suddenly became aware of something. I realized that my approach was a bit high-flying, transhistorical in some ways. So I began to look for inspiration in the Colt revolver. Originally, all these things were part of a reflection on the idea of resistance. I tried to write a little book about Pure War and its consequences, which would echo the preceding one.

That's what you began in Popular Defense and Ecological Struggles.

Yes. The second part, furthermore—"Revolutionary Resistance"—is a paradox: to my mind, there is no more revolution except in resistance.

This means reviving the logic of the brake. Is nothing to be expected of acceleration?

At that point, I came across a phrase of Kipling's: "The first casualty of war is truth." The first victim of speed as war is truth. I suddenly understood that the importance of speed in the war phenomenon is also a phenomenon of world-vision, in the strict sense: television is a phenomenon of speed, a vision resulting from speed. That led me to become more and more interested in the cinema. At the moment I'm preparing an essay for *Cahiers du Cinéma* on "War and Cinema," to show to what extent the essence of war and the essence of film are related.

The cinema is war pursued by other means.

It's not by chance that the movie camera was preceded by Marey's chrono-photographic rifle and the Gatling gun, which was itself inspired by the Colt revolver. All these things are at the origin of war. At the moment, then, I'm fairly involved in the phenomena of speed and representation: how—through audio-visuals, through the press, through the media—does war perpetuate itself in "emoting-power"?

As we saw before, emoting-power is the impact of speed on the senses, the emotional extension of dromological "moving-power."

I have gone from moving-power to emoting-power through the vision of the world. This means that, next to the speed of light—which everyone knows since it organized world perspective—there is the light of speed.

What's "moving" about speed is that it makes things visible.

In the theory of relativity, the speed of light is considered universally impassable: 186,000 miles/second. It seems to me that, in a parallel way, this speed of light is also a light of speed. All speed illuminates. The low speeds of Victor Hugo's train, the relatively high speeds of the Concorde, or the very high speeds of televised projection are electronic or thermodynamic light—thermodynamic light in the case of the train, light of the reactor in the Concorde, and electronic light in television. When one is on a jet or on a train, one sees the world in a different light, so to speak. It's not the problem of light source, but of relation to the world. The world flown over is a world produced by speed. It's a representation. We come back to Schopenhauer's pessimism, the world as representation, but this time as representation of speed.

And this world produced by speed is cinema.

The world becomes a cinema. It's this effect of speed on the landscape that I called a *dromoscopy*, in the strict sense. We speak of stroboscopy, in other words the effects induced by an energy and a relation of observation on an object. But this stroboscopy is also a dromoscopy. What happens in the train window, in the car windshield, in the television screen, is the same kind of cinematism. We have gone from the aesthetics of appearance, stable forms, to the aesthetics of disappearance, unstable forms.

How would you characterize this passage, this appearance-disappearance, in terms of aesthetics?

Appearance or disappearance, it's all sleight of hand. It's what happens in movies. The aesthetics of painting (with respect to the aesthetics of film) rely on appearance. The painter paints and the sketch appears, until the image is fixed and varnished. By contrast, film images are present insofar as they flash by at twenty-four images/second. They are present because they vanish quickly. They give an impression of movement because they disappear as soon as they are perceived. They exist because they are unstable, because they escape. There we have an inversion of the pictorial aesthetics of appearance into the aesthetics of disappearance, a photo-cinemato-video-holographic aesthetic.

I'm reminded of something Jean Baudrillard said: "It's not enough to die, you still have to disappear…" Is every disappearance nonetheless bound to make something reappear—or is there a threshold beyond which images themselves slip away?

There is, of course, the possibility of disappearance in excessive speed: disappearance of the world's peculiarities and of the consciousness we could have of them to the extent that overaccelerated speed renders us unconscious.

That's the subliminal effect we talked about.

Yes. If we go to five hundred images/second, to a million images/second (and there are already machines that allow this), we see *nothing*. Too much speed is comparable to too much light. It's blinding.

Isn't Speed and Politics *a misleading, or at least paradoxical, title? If speed is what is beyond representation as politics, speed is therefore beyond politics or, as they say now, it's the end of politics. Exceeding politics, speed blinds it. Speed and politics form a couple which really isn't one, a couple which destroys itself. Unless that's precisely the role of the couple.*

It's a couple that destroys itself. Only it destroyed itself not so long ago. The production of speed is a recent event: it goes back to the beginning of the nineteenth century. The political career, on the other hand, is enormous; it covers millennia. Before politics was a matter of appearances. Greek civilization tried to promote an image of the world through culture, philosophy, strategy, through "poliorcetics," the art of defending the city—an art invented by the Greeks, don't forget. Etymologically, the urbanist is a man who builds cities in order to defend them. And to defend a city today, one must act upon a point of inertia, that is, on its azimuthal projection into the space-time of speed and communications. But the serious problem is that those present, those who participate, those, for example, who attend an auto race are disqualified by the absentees. The billion people who watch the Olympic Games in Moscow, or the soccer championship in Argentina, impose their power at the expense of those present, who are already superfluous. The latter are practically no more than bodies filling the stadium so that it won't look empty. But their physical presence is completely alienated by the absence of the television viewer. There's a complete inversion, and that's what interests me in this situation. Once the stadiums were full. It was a magnificent popular explosion. There were two hundred thousand people in the grandstands, singing and shouting. It was a vision from ancient society, from the agora, from paganism. Now when you watch the Olympics or the soccer championship on television, you notice there aren't that many people. And even they, in a certain way, aren't the ones who make the World Cup. The ones who make the World Cup are the radios and televisions that buy and—by favoring a billion and a half television viewers—"produce" the championship. Those absent from the stadium are always right, economically and massively. They have the power. The participants are always wrong.

And the "absentees" in South America?

Not the same. On one hand, disappearance is linked to repression. On the other, it's linked to the technological space, which is not a geographical space, but a space of time. When I say that the absentees are right, I mean that they are there. They aren't in the place itself, but they are there in time, which is the time of worldwide broadcasting. So today, concentration in the space of a city or a stadium corresponds to a concentration in broadcasting time. Broadcasting replaces urbanization. It's a city of the instant in which a billion people are gathered. Which is already an image of polar inertia. And so disappearance is on one hand the tragic disappearance of people killed or reduced, degraded to the point of no longer knowing their own identities: this is repression by the Latin American secret police. And then there's the same disappearance in the parceling out of time required to broadcast an event.

This isn't merely inversion. This is polar inertia, which makes television viewers inert. They are citizens of the world, but relativized. In South America, on the other hand, people vanish into thin air, but their inertia is not part of the technical apparatus itself. It's police liquidation, pure and simple.

There are qualitative differences. This phenomenon nonetheless sheds light on terrorist practices as well as on the State terrorism that developed in South America with the technique of disappearances. No longer the practice of the concentration camps, of German-style enclosure, but the disappearance of people. Sleight of hand. Social magic. It's the society of disappearance.

What do you mean exactly by "society of disappearance?"

Until the Second World War—until the concentration camps—societies were societies of incarceration, of imprisonment in the Foucauldian sense. The great transparency of the world, whether through satellites or simply tourists, brought about an overexposure of these places to observation, to the press and public opinion which now ban concentration camps. You can't isolate anything in this world of ubiquity and instantaneousness. Even if some camps still exist, this overexposure of the world led to the need to surpass enclosure and imprisonment. This required the promotion of another kind of repression, which is disappearance. (Gangsters had already invented it by making bodies disappear in cement.) On this level, South America was one more laboratory for the politics of disappearance.

The original forms of military repression in Latin America are highly "exportable" to Western countries. In fact, they come from there. Latin America is to American imperialism what Spain was to Nazi Germany: an opportunity to test its new technology cheaply.

Many people don't realize to what extent disappearance is not a complementary technique, but one which is becoming central.

Bodies must disappear. People don't exist. There is a big future in this technology because it's so similar to what happened in the history of war. In war, we've seen how important disappearance, camouflage, dissimulation are—every war is a war of cunning. You remember what Kipling said about the first casualty.

Now there are no more casualties. Only desaparecidos, *the missing.*

The disappearance of people now happens in civilian society with the secret police.

It's also another concept of the State. Traditionally, the State is power on exhibit, power that shows its face. It's the gravitas, *pomp and circumstance, the solemnity of power in representation. Here, on the contrary, the State absorbs techniques of the nomad war-machine, the secret of the warrior who takes advantage of the surprise-effect to win. The urban guerrilla also uses camouflage, but his actions must be as spectacular as possible in hopes of rousing the masses and shaking the State's power. The only true terrorism, in short, is State terrorism, as it isn't answerable to anybody for its actions.*

The State has become suicidal. In the beginning, it didn't have the means. Now it does, whence the politics of disappearance. Whence Cambodia. When I wrote "The Suicide State," Cambodia hadn't happened yet. Which proves I was right, that the State can be completely eliminated, that disappearance can go all the way to the end.

9

Endo-colonization and
the State-as-Destiny

Ecologistics and Nondevelopment □ Auschwitz, Hiroshima, Cambodia □ Endo-colonization □ The End of Ideology □ Africa, Latin America, United States □ Welfare-State and the State-as-Destiny □ The Quality of the Instant □ The Delusion of Self-management □ Absolute Deregulation

Let's come back to the superseding of the Nation-States, which led people to conceive of the end of politics—the end, shall we say, of a period of growth and progress in civilian societies. How did we end up with such an inversion?

If we can say that war was entirely strategy in past societies, if strategy governed the Nation-States at the beginning of the twentieth century, we can now say that strategy is no more than logistics. In turn, logistics has become the whole of war; because in an age of deterrence, the production of arms is already war.

Deterrence, then, doesn't mean to ensure peace, but rather to settle into war.

Deterrence is the development of an arms capacity that assures total peace. The fact of having increasingly sophisticated weaponry deters the enemy more and more. At that point, war is no longer in its execution, but in its preparation. The perpetuation of war is what I call Pure War, war which isn't acted out in repetition, but in infinite preparation. Only this infinite preparation, the advent of logistics, also entails the nondevelopment of society in the sense of civilian consumption.

The age of deterrence completely transforms the nature of war: direct confrontation becomes scarce, but civilian society pays the price of its infinite postponement. And yet, hasn't it always been the case? Before civilian society was bled dry by war, now it's crushed to death by peace. War can always change character. That tendency, at least, remains the same.

In the past, the execution of war was an exchange—brutal, of course, and enormously draining, but strictly relative with respect to civilian economy. With the development of the war economy, we saw an inversion. Now, with the development of deterrence— not only the "all-points" strategy of the 1950s and 1960s, but also the "all-weapons" strategy of the 1970s and 1980s—we're heading toward a generalized nondevelopment which, in terms of war economy, is similar to zero growth in ecological terms. The notion of ecological zero growth corresponds to zero growth in "ecologistics."

What do you mean by "ecologistics"?

I mean the development of an overall logistics: of rockets and all-points missiles as well as the conventional weapons supposedly necessitated by the Soviet adversary, which builds thousands upon thousands of tanks, strengthens its naval power considerably, and tends to fully develop both the traditional and exceptional aspects of war. That war economy promotes the nondevelopment of civilian societies is not only true of the Third World, as some tend to think, but also of the "middle power" countries of Europe; hence the debate currently raging over Euro-missiles. Eventually it will also be true of the United States. I won't mention the Soviets, since they refused to follow the path of civilian consumption long ago. Remember that it was Eisenhower, when he left the White House, who denounced the military-industrial complex that he himself had helped create (probably because of his religious beliefs: he wanted to confess his sins before dying). Immediately afterward, we had Maxwell Taylor's theory on the *uncertain trumpet*, the "flexible response"—in other words on the need to develop conventional weapons alongside strategic nuclear weapons. At about the same time—all this happened within a space of several years— Nikita Khrushchev found himself in direct contact with the head military official, Zhukov or Malinovsky, and was dismissed because he wanted to promote civilian consumption in the USSR in order to catch up with the United States. Khrushchev knew that American imperialism could only be fought on the grounds of an imperialism of the Soviet way of life. They couldn't keep developing military institutions and still claim that Soviet imperialism would be attractive to future societies. Khrushchev wanted to stay with all-points strategy. It would be enough to perfect the great thermo-nuclear vectors, and then develop civilian society. The Soviet military class said: "No, it's out of the question." You can see how nondevelopment is at the very center of transpolitics.

Marx spoke of a pauperization of the working class—which never happened, furthermore, since the proletariat has been absorbed by bourgeois society, and with it the reality of class struggle. What we see now is a relative pauperization of civilian society in favor of military society. The zero growth of civilian society goes hand in hand with the absolute growth of the military state.

Absolutely. Moreover, along with deterrence, there's an extraordinary inversion which we haven't analyzed yet: the military establishments (the a-national military class) no longer opposes anything but civilian societies—its own civilian societies. For me, there were three exemplary events: the first was Auschwitz; the second, Hiroshima; the third, Cambodia. What happened in Cambodia was a scale model, a schema, a caricature of what's happening on a world-wide scale. The military class is turning into an internal super-police. Moreover, it's logical. In the strategy of deterrence, military institutions, no longer fighting among themselves, tend to fight only civilian societies—with, of course, a few skirmishes in the Third World (the role of the police played here and there by Europe—particularly France, and elsewhere by the United States at the time of Vietnam).

The South American secret police, the death squads we were talking about before, are not simply a flaw of anachronistic, dictatorial regimes. It's the future of national armies, their new trade. Economic bloodsucking, in short, doesn't spare the lives of populations: we've gained nothing in the exchange.

In ancient society, in which economic and political strategies dominated, the army was a national defense; its job was to protect borders, or to expand them by fighting the enemy. In the society of national security—the term itself is quite interesting—the armed forces turn against their own populations: on the one hand to exact the funds necessary for Pure War, the infinite development of their weaponry (through very precise forms of political pressure—as we can easily see in France, where it works even on a Socialist government); and on the other to control society. What's happening in Poland today is similar to what happened in Cambodia, even if there are differences: turning a state of war into a war against one's own population.

It's the colonization of one's own territory.

It's no longer exo-colonization (the age of extending world conquest), but the age of intensiveness and endo-colonization. One now colonizes only one's own population. One underdevelops one's own civilian economy.

Paradoxically, the rise of the military in the Third World is not an archaism, but a prefiguration of what's in store for Western societies.

Absolutely. South America, and also Africa to a certain extent, are the laboratories of future society, one in which control and colonization will be carried out by the country's own forces of order—often with the help of foreign armies. It's what happened in 1947 with the Inter-American Treaty on Reciprocal Assistance, which was supposed to prevent foreign intervention and thus coagulate the populations. We see what it really allows them to do: it allows the Argentines to step in and support the take-over by General Meza, the drug-general (it's important to remember that).

It allows the Honduran armed forces inside the "Iron Triangle" to lend a hand, along with Guatemala, to the Salvadoran forces against Salvadoran peasants. We can see the perversions of traditional defense systems quite well.

Furthermore, another perversion of the traditional distinctions is produced: the military's direct rise to power occurs in the name of ideologies which are indifferently reactionary or socialist, as with Portugal, Chile, Cambodia, and Peru.

The ideology of the Peruvian, Portuguese, Spanish, or even Polish generals is irrelevant. We're no longer in a system dominated by ideology. We're in a system in which military order dominates. The only ideology is order. No matter if that order is socialist, capitalist or anything else, so long as it's not really political but military.

It's another way of defining the end of politics.

It's another regulation. It's no longer a regulation of parties, a political or even social regulation, but a "non-party" regulation—in other words, by the military police. There are obviously variants for each situation, but it's still interesting to see that in most of the countries we've taken as examples, in Latin America or Africa, as in the Soviet Union, the army is a means—in fact, the only means—of social promotion.

Since you mention it, we've barely spoken about Africa. Is the African continent just as subject to military police-style regulation as Latin America?

I recently learned that Argentina's debt alone equaled that of the entire African continent. Something like that seems very mysterious to me, but it explains why I've always been more interested in Latin American underdevelopment than in African underdevelopment. Africa seems impermeable, and in the final account not very representative of the effects of Western technology. On the other hand, it seems that Latin America bears the effects of an extraordinary perversity which could certainly act as analytical instruments. Europe dominated Latin America, it colonized the South American continent before the United States. But I believe Europe's future lies in Latin America. Latin America prefigures Europe's fate just as the Balkans are the equivalent of Latin America for the Soviet Union. I'm sure that eventually (and the current situation with exchange rates confirms this) America's allies will have no other choice but to become the Brazil or the Argentina—not to mention Uruguay and El Salvador—of the Capital-State's central continent (capitals aren't cities, they're States including suburbs and countryside).

As far as the United States is concerned, Reagan's "deregulatory" policies, like the colossal increase of the American military budget, are slowly tracing the outline of this kind of armed State.

As I see it, Reaganism is already endo-colonization applied to America. The Welfare State which existed in Europe, and to a certain extent in the United States during the 1960s, is being replaced in the US by what I call a State-as-destiny. This means that we're entering the "State of inevitability"—nuclear inevitability, technological inevitability, and other kinds.

In England the Welfare State nonetheless continues to be very strong. This in part forestalls the arrival of the State-as-destiny, but not of economic collapse. So either they punish the populations directly, as in the United States, or else it's the total decline of the nation's power when the Welfare State is maintained at a certain degree of intensity. Either way you lose.

The Welfare State is inscribed in a vision of time and history which is completely different from the State-as-destiny. The Welfare State is the State that makes things last, that thinks of history as duration—long duration. Now, I think all that is over. The end of politics is the end of history. We're entering a trans-political vision in which it's the intensity of the instant that counts. There are two kinds of time: an extensive, historical time (from pre-history until now) and an intensive time, that of the state of emergency—in the generic sense, of course—where what counts is the quality of the instant. I was recently at the Avoriaz colloquium on science fiction film. What surprised me is that, along with the prizes for best actor, best screenplay, etc., they're now going to give a prize for the best minute—the most intense minute. In my view, that's an illustration of something prefiguring the politics of the minimum-State. It will no longer be important to last, but to "get a thrill"—the quality of life will depend on the intensity of the instant, and not the stability of duration.

The minimal State is also the State-as-destiny. Are we now condemned to getting a thrill for nothing—and before long, from nothing? Obviously, nothing can equal the intensity of the nuclear instant....

The maximum politics of the Welfare State is succeeded by a minimal politics—a minimum-State, as Milton Friedman's neoconservatives say. A minimum-State means a pauperization, in my view, and more precisely: endo-colonization. It would seem that societies have lost their capacity for self-regulation. This capacity is now in the hands of the multinationals, but not from underneath. Underneath there is no longer any possibility for a rebirth of the individual. This might still exist on the level of certain small cultural practices, but on the productive level, there are no groups capable of regulating themselves.

We already raised this question indirectly, when talking about Italian Autonomy. You praised them for having invented the question, but it's evident that for you, group self-management, at the point we've reached, is not a viable response.

I don't believe in the kind of self-management they're talking about in Europe. I hope for self-management, the group's capacity for autonomy. I'm in favor of direct democracy, I think it's wonderful—but idealistic and utopian. It's a desire—before the foreboding of nondevelopment and a deregulation by the military State, by Pure War, by maximum investment in the production of the war-machine—for turning to the past, toward self-regulation of a communal, tribal society. To my mind, it's an enormous retrogressive illusion. I can't forget that this desire for self-management coexists with a desire for hyper-centralization, which is the result of technology. Why is there at this time a "back and forth" movement between the left and the right about self-regulation? It's because a Pure State is coming about, a World State which is simultaneously tied in with nuclear power, with the coupling of Russia and America on the strategic level and with the economic coupling of capitalism and the other countries. Just look at what happened in Poland with the World Bank… There is a de facto congruence, an inertia of military power which joins the two blocs and furthermore, with the multinationals, a tendency toward the unity of world economy, as we have an economy of nuclear deterrence. So I'm for people "regulating" themselves, but I can't forget that the Pure State, the single, universal State of the Fascists (I'm thinking of *The Universal State*, a manifesto by Ernst Jünger) means the multinationals. The multinationals are spreading all over the world, while becoming all the more concentrated on the economic and financial level. The multinationals' industrial redeployment is a retrogressive phenomenon comparable to deurbanization. What did they do? They exploited the entire World. They put people to work in Hong Kong, Cameroon, etc. And at the same time they became concentrated. There's simply a return effect. It's what happened on the industrial level, and it's now happening on the urban level. The same phenomenon of spreading, of urban redistribution, conceals an even stronger concentration of the deciding structures. An even greater capitalization is produced, but of a different nature—it becomes like a control tower or a bank terminal. I'm not defending the city, I'm defending the unity of space and time. Before banks, it was capital. The city was a bank. It built ramparts: that was the safe deposit box. Today the safe is the place in which information, givens are concentrated. Thus a hyper-concentration of economic and military power. In answer to hyper-concentration, we need a hyper-deregulation. So to my mind, overtures made at this time to self-management area trap, leading toward a "do-it-yourself" situation, toward the abandonment of all social politics. From this point of view, Reagan's politics are ahead of the times: you concentrate power on war, on economic and military-industrial development, etc., and you let the rest drop dead. This comes down to saying: "Manage yourselves, do what you want, take care of your own sexual customs, do your thing in life, and we'll take care of the rest."

In the United States, in fact, autonomy, far from being an ultra-leftist movement, is a catchword of right-wing individualism. It's the right to arm yourself to the teeth to protect your property, ensure your survival in case of social collapse, etc. Actually, what I was trying to do in the issue of Semiotext(e) *devoted to "Autonomia" was define its Italian context.*[10]

Today, we can't hear a demand for autonomy without hearing "social disintegration" at the same time. Not a diaspora of regained freedom, of tribal or rural societies, of the famous self-managed, self-regulated commune, etc.; but rather the absolute deregulation of absolute inertia. Power is centered to the maximum on a strong point, where the Russians and the Americans are joined as well as the multinationals and the socialistic state capitalism of the Eastern countries. And all the rest is deregulation. We can all drop dead. In any case, they no longer need us: robots and computers will take care of production. War is automatized, and along with it the power of decision. They no longer need men, soldiers, or workers, only means of absolute extermination, on the commercial level as elsewhere.

State terrorism is a form of self-management which has gone from the individual to the state level. It's not peace one administers, but one's own war.

Absolutely.

10

The Production of Destruction

Evacuating the Cities □ Pol Pot □ The Economy of Destiny □
Marxism and War □ The Paris Commune □ The A-politics of
the Worst □ Facing Death □ Popular Resistance □ Woman and
Warrior □ Terrorism and Technology □ Nuclear Blackmail and
Deurbanization □ Dividing Lines

*Next to nuclear mythology—which can be quite real and threatening—
we now have the science fiction of war. I'm thinking of the procedures
for population evacuation outlined in the Reagan Plan.*

The seven-year plan.

*Can we find an equivalent elsewhere, in the USSR for example? Is
this something new in the preparation for permanent war?*

Yes. We can distinguish two systems: the system of defense against
an enemy, and the system of security against a threat. These two
systems are quite different on the epistemological level. Defense and
the enemy built territories, temporalities of all kinds, whether they
were the Latin American *cuadras*, the city of Miletus or the Roman

centuriations. Inversely, security and threats dismantled territories. This is the case with the seven-year plan. What will it do? Cities will be evacuated, a diaspora provoked, territories disorganized. It's deregulation. The threat's hypothetical and completely phantasmic nature in the doctrine of national security contributes toward the disintegration of territory—and not only of territory. In the name of security, in the name of protection, everything is undone, deregulated: economic relations, social relations, sexual relations, relations of money and power. We end up in a state of defeat, without there ever having been a war.

And strangely enough, the metaphor for this deregulation of territory is again Cambodia, but on the archaic side.

Absolutely. Cambodia is the scale-model of the suicide State which no longer gathers populations in order to exploit territory, but which infinitely dissolves it. If they had let Pol Pot act as he saw fit, there would have been no one left. It was Robespierre, the Terror spread over an entire country. It would have meant Cambodia's disappearance. There wouldn't even have been any more executioners. A cartoon from 1793 symbolized the end of the Terror in France by the image of an executioner guillotining himself. That image was Cambodia.

At the same time, the Cambodian experience happened in the perspective of opposition to technology, against its importation to the Third World.

It happened in the name of Marxism—in other words, of an industrious technology, not an industrial one. Marxism and technocracy have curious contacts. They're not the same thing (even if there are Marxist-Stalinist technocrats), but they unquestionably influence each other.

Jean Baudrillard speaks about the end of the age of production. Does this correspond to the transfer of technological production, the logic of destructive means, into the domain of Pure War?

It's what I call a revolution in the means of destruction. First there was a revolution in the modes of production, the illusion of progress through technology and science. Now that is over. The revolution which appears within the revolution in modes of production is its opposite. As Admiral Sevestre (the editor of the French National Defense organ) says, "Industrial production must be coherent with military production." This statement perfectly represents the revolution in modes of destruction. It's the absolute identification of production with destruction.

The production of war is general economy in the sense Georges Bataille gives it. And industrial production is no more than restricted economy....

The revolution in means of production is the economy of destiny. War is organized, but somehow it always escapes which leads to the current escape, the escape of nuclear war, of deterrence.

Marxism has largely obscured the function of war by making it the consequence of economics, and not its origin.

To my mind, there was some hocus-pocus between Marx and Engels. Engels was aware of the reality of war, even if he didn't see it the way we do. There was also the idea of war as reappropriated by the working class. The working class, especially at the beginning of trade unionism, was a combat unit. This relation of Marxism to war wasn't really clear at the outset. Let's not talk about today…

Marxism has always been a war-machine. But in the service of…

In the service of… Never mind. In that sense, I feel closer to the Commune. The Paris Commune, which Marx used as a model, wasn't a war-machine—far from it, even if it owed its birth in large part to the Franco-Prussian War. I feel rather close to the Communards, even if as a Christian I can't go along with their practice of slaughtering priests. It was a social revolt which refused war. Thus the conflict between the two generals of the Paris Commune, who wanted to organize a popular war, and the Communards who didn't, who wanted it to be the people's war, a war without strategy. And this brings into play things that concern socialism, in the "peasant" sense of the word: socialism would be a continuation of peasant guerrilla warfare by other means—and not a passage to industrial war and everything else Marxism will bring.

Do you mean that the State, even the Marxist state, is bound to re-institutionalize war?

Inevitably. Just look at Trotsky's role. He was a first-rate figure in matters of war.

Recently in the US a debate was initiated on the confusion that occurred between the civilians and the military around the building of the first military shuttle. When they began considering investing capital and technology in military industry, they declared: "We will take elements from civilian industry, but in no way will we confuse the two." It was already a recognition of their confusion that showed in this denial. Another question we could raise at this point concerns the effect that this transfer of technology to Third World countries could have on traditional societies, insofar as it pushes toward a process of territorial disintegration. Paradoxically, this connects with the problem of Cambodia, where the refusal of technology led to a comparable disintegration. How can we explain such a bizarre merging of two such contradictory choices? After all, even if they acted like savages, the people of Phnom-Penh remained within the limits you describe.

Except that I don't believe we can refuse technology, go back to Year One, so to speak. We can't stop everything to give ourselves time for reflection. I believe it's within the inquiry into technology that we'll find, not a solution, but the possibility of a solution. That's why I'm so interested in the war-machine. Hölderlin's phrase: "But where the danger grows, grows also that which saves," is very important to me. I believe that within this perversion of human knowledge by the war-machine, hides its opposite. Thus there is work to be done within the machine itself, and in my view politics has never done anything other than this. Politics, in the ancient sense of the invention of the political, has never done anything other than put its hands in the bloody guts of the cadaver of war, and pull out something that could be used—something that wasn't war. Today the military knows all about civilians, but civilians know nothing about the military. For me, this is the worst possible situation. *That's* the Apolitics of the Worst. Politics, on the contrary, means facing this tendency toward extremes, this enemy, this false priest, in order to question it—as in a struggle with the angels, or with the devil. It's the question of death: we can't escape it, we must face it intellectually and physically, as doctors and artists have. When we see Leonardo da Vinci's discovery of death, we realize just how much the Renaissance artists—and later Delacroix, Gericault, and Soutine were fascinated by corpses. There we have a will, which is not at all morbid, to confront death. They were fascinated by death as they were fascinated by waterfalls, by lightning, by storms. And I believe it's the same thing today. We must get inside Pure War, we must cover ourselves with blood and tears. We mustn't turn away. *That* is political and civil virtue.

That could explain the fascination you've been accused of feeling for the military and for death. Just as death has been repressed, they would repress war as well.

Yes. One is civilian only insofar as one is not afraid. If the civilian is characterized by his cowardice at confronting situations, then he's really what the military wishes him to be. In that case, it's the military that assumes the courageous role: "Live in peace, my brothers; live in peace, my women; I will confront death for you." "Thanks, dad, I'll do it myself"—that's my reaction. The racket, no thank you. We don't need the State. We certainly don't need to be protected from wondering about something which is a condition of our existence: death. Death of the individual, death of the species. Because *that's* the military's justification. An old argument. Therefore, I say we're really in civilian life when we confront the question of death. Whence my interest in popular defense: how each man is able to take on his own defense. I'll give you a simple example. About ten of us had gotten together to prepare for the trial of a soldier who had gone AWOL. Some members of the Ordre Nouveau (a fascist group) attacked us with shovel handles, and they broke my arm. Everyone said, "Let's go to the cops." Only one person didn't go, and that was me. It seemed ridiculous to ask the police to defend us. You go home; you draw your own conclusions. No way we can go to the cops! I was only annoyed at not having foreseen our being attacked. On that level, I feel very close to the peasants. The peasants are real civilians....

The peasants are disappearing... Is popular defense still possible against the exponential development of armaments?

No. Popular defense uses the milieu, it doesn't use the means. Guerrillas can defend themselves because they're in a milieu they know perfectly, admirably. They don't need extraordinary weapons. The peasants had pitchforks, tools, slingshots—and that was enough. As soon as there's an enormous diaspora, as soon as the peasants become city-dwellers, and the city-dwellers themselves are dispersed in their sociality, scattered over the face of the earth (precisely because we're in geopolitics, and no longer in politics), nothing remains with which to defend oneself. All that remains is the single individual and his deterritorialization. He can't do anything. And there you have a panic situation that leads to the end of popular resistance. Already, the strike was the beginning of an answer to this, a way of saying: "We can't set up barricades, we'll interrupt elsewhere than in space. Space is all yours; we'll defend ourselves in time, by shutdowns, interruptions, wildcat strikes, refusal to pay taxes." But it's not enough. Right now, the situation of popular resistance is very grim.

Popular resistance is in a crisis because the people have lost their "ground," which was both their milieu and their base of operations. But along with the earth, their social, familial, and tribal unity also disappears.

Women's liberation led to the defeat of the logistical couple: the original war-machine is a man and a woman. The couple is not only good for making babies. Marriage is in reality a war-machine, not a machine of production. Women allowed man to become a real warrior. Every man said: "Don't look at death, I'll do it; you cook for me." We see the same system today with technocracy and the formless masses: "Above all, don't look at death, we'll take care of it; you work." Always the same story, except that man did it long before there were proletarian masses.

So women liberation produces a new warrior.

Yes, a new warrior, except that I don't really see how it could work in a system of popular defense.

War is no longer founded on the division of the sexes.

No, of course not. But the diaspora I was talking about before, the diaspora of the sexes, does not favor unarmed struggle. Why did I say that popular defense (more than guerrilla warfare) was interesting? Because it used the milieu, because it was in an economy of the means of the society being defended, and even a domestic economy in the context of man and woman. As soon as you cut that off, you're forced to use arms. Which is what happens with terrorism. They manage to stay within a technocratic situation, for example a plane, a car, a train, a boat. They take out their big P.38

revolver, and because they're in a moving vehicle which people can't get out of, you have a situation of force. They begin using weapons, and do exactly what the military has done. They need a means, then an industry to procure these means, in the end it becomes Pure War. That's the short cut. The terrorist who says: "My women took off, my kids are illegitimate (not one of them would recognize me), my parents can't stand me (they're too bourgeois), so I'll get a big pistol, get on a Boeing, and get down to it"—that terrorist becomes a military man. It's no longer popular defense!

That was the conclusion reached by Hans-Joachim Klein, the German terrorist now in hiding. He recognized that armed struggle wasn't popular defense, but the "politics of massacre."[11]

Even if he's Palestinian and has all sorts of justifications which I recognize, I still have to say that the system is totally perverse. I think: "They're starting up again." The terrorist has to have a weapons industry, because if the weapons industry stopped, there would be no more terrorists. Let's assume that tomorrow there are no more P.38 manufacturers, that the Boeings are grounded by strikes, that there's no more fuel, no more cars, no more machines: terrorism would be finished. Terrorism is intimately connected with technologization. In this sense it's no popular defense, even if they think it is.

For William Burroughs, the difference between a CIA agent and a member of the Italian Red Brigades is that one is part of an official club, and the other simply a putterer.

Absolutely—an amateur.

Let's come back to the question of domestic economy. Do loss of sexual identity, social fragmentation, and individual atomization mean that this attempt at liberation simultaneously contributes to war?

I am quite interested in women's liberation. Luce Irigaray[12] is a very old friend of mine, and I like the research she's doing into female identity very much: it's the will to manifest an identity which would not be known, which would be revealed in its absolute originality. It's a mad and passionate experiment, which, to my mind, resembles the invention of dietary customs. We must have begun like that. Culture came out of a similar will to create difference. Aside from this marvellous invention, which I support entirely, the political dimension of the women's liberation movement is shot, as far as I can tell. Because they don't take into account the geopolitical dimension, the situation of Pure War, of absolute deterrence that we now know.

They end up creating more cops under the banner of liberation.

Absolutely! And especially, to free ourselves, we must do without everything that surrounds us. For example, I find Nicaragua great. It has its revolution, fine, almost a good popular defense, they manage to create a society which isn't a complete copy of the Soviet model. And then a year or two later, it's the State of emergency. For Nicaragua really to be free, they would have to free everything else! There we have the problem of the International all over again. It was the tragedy of Marxism, but it's also the tragedy of all liberation movements. If all of us aren't liberated at the same time, it serves no purpose whatsoever. I have no global answer or unifying vision of what must be done. I only have questions, clips, glimpses. Always fractals.

Let's come back to the Reagan Plan. Local collectives vigorously opposed the very notion of civil defense. "We refuse to install these devices," they said, "even shelters, because it would mean making the very idea of nuclear war acceptable." Do you believe this military-science fiction screenplay is truly applicable? The New Yorker's first reaction is to say that any project for evacuating cities, no matter how it's done, is impossible.

Certainly. But what's hidden behind that? The weapon is always an alibi. The nuclear goddess dominates, but she's not really active; she's simply the center of the spider web. I believe that the Reagan Plan is not really intended to answer an atomic warning. *It's intended to condition populations,* and especially to prepare them for endo-colonization. Cities don't allow endo-colonization: they have to die. Cities correspond to a civil status, to citizenship, to the appearance of politics in a space which opposes endo-colonization. Only look at the steps taken by the Jesuits when they came to the *reducciones* (settlements). The first thing they did was to destroy the tribal structure by scattering the village, by giving it a layout which had nothing to do with what had previously existed. Which meant that the natives were lost. I think the Reagan Plan is of the same order as what the Jesuits did, but this time it spreads to rearranging the American territory. For me, the future is deurbanization. The Reagan Plan is only possible if one is aware (and I am an urbanist) that the future is the end of the cities; it's the suburbs; it's the defeat of urban integration in favor of a megasuburb. Not the megalopolis, the megasuburb.

Paradoxically, this plan of deurbanization ties in with certain of the Italian Autonomists' intuitions. The decentralization of industries means the end of working-class concentrations, and thus the end of the proletariat. But the Italians see this spreading of production as having positive aspects as well.

You can't force the people to leave the cities. But if you stress the fact that the Pershings, SS-20's, missiles, etc., could fall at any moment on the great urban centers, people start thinking seriously of moving to the country. The nuclear threat makes you swallow anything. It's racket logic!

Nuclear blackmail ties in with and reinforces tendencies already active in our society. With the end of the age of production, we are seeing the disappearance of the territorial bases of workers' identity. Technology can now work in fragments, in geographical dispersal, as with the "cottage industries."

Space is no longer in geography—it's in electronics. Unity is in the terminals. It's in the instantaneous time of command posts, multi-national headquarters, control towers, etc. Politics is less in physical space than in the time systems administered by various technologies, from telecommunications to airplanes, passing by the TGV [French high-speed train], etc. There is a movement from geo- to chronopolitics: the distribution of territory becomes the distribution of time. The distribution of territory is outmoded, minimal.

In The Third Wave, *Alvin Tofler describes the scattering of industries over the entire territory as an aspect of technological progress. American reindustrialization doesn't go by way of the rectification of previous structures, but by way of generalized scattering and the advent of a "sunken" economy, as the Italians call it.*

Exactly. World unity is no longer a spatial unity. For territory, the unit of measure is distances in time. Every day we invent new time measurements, cognitive measurements: milliseconds, nanoseconds. That's where it all happens; politics is now in that kind of measurement, as we agreed before. The Pharaohs, the Romans, the Greeks were surveyors. That was geopolitics. We're no longer there, we're in chronopolitics. Organization, prohibitions, interruptions, orders, powers, structurings, subjections are now in the realm of temporality. And that's also where resistance should be. If we fight in space instead of fighting in time, it's like meeting Ray Bradbury's characters in *The Martian Chronicles*, who are there without being there.

What strikes me is that what you're saying completely ties in with economists' and urbanists' predictions concerning technological evolution and the benefits our civilization should reap from it.

Except that I don't believe in these benefits.

Don't you sometimes think you're recreating a universality, a somewhat paranoid vision of things? Does the world of technology force us to adopt this viewpoint?

No. I was a man of enclosures. I'm very sensitive to limits, to inter-ruptions—interfaces, if you prefer. It's not by chance that I studied the Atlantic Wall. I didn't study the blockhouses, I studied their position. I studied the wall, the circle of blockhouses, every-thing that happens between the continental space and the maritime space. Later I went to see the Siegfried Line and the Maginot Line, but after the Atlantic Wall: I never would have wanted to go beforehand. It's because I was interested in the coastal region. For me, the coastal region is an amazing thing, a marvellous interruption, an interface, as they say. I've always thought of space in terms of breaks, in terms of either/or, in terms of the dividing line of waters—those places where things are exchanged, transformed. Chronopolitics and the distribution of time—that's the level I see them on, not on the level of expanse. Expanse is less important than the point at which things change, at which there is a fragment.

Why do dividing lines interest you?

Because they multiply the fragments, they multiply the interfaces, they multiply what is not neutral. The continent and the sea exist thanks to the coastal area. And that's a very interesting ambivalence. So I prefer not to describe the situation we're discussing as "tragic," "paranoid," etc. I never use these terms, except for nuclear arms and war.

11

The War-Machine and Death

The Fatal Couple □ SALT, START: Limitation or Sophistication of Weapons? □ The Future of Pacifism □ Missile and Messiah □ Nuclear Power and the Return of the Sacred □ The Question of Death □ Death and Political Awareness □ Capital Punishment □ Disappearance of the Law □ Death Between the Civilian and the Military □ The Question of God □ Suicide of the Race

It's becoming more and more obvious that the confrontation of blocs guarantees the coupling of the two rival imperialisms. "Evil in our time," as Reagan says, is not Russia, but the rivalry itself which serves the two powers' respective interests.

We cannot understand the phenomenon of the ultimate weapon outside of the deterrent couple. To cut one part off and say that the first ones are horrible and the second pitiful is only a way of avoiding the situation.

It still means putting ideology first. And these days, ideology only serves to justify ambitions of hegemony.

Absolutely. I think that what's been instituted is a fatal coupling between the US and the USSR. The arms race unifies them. Furthermore, I said it in my first book, *L'insécurité du Territoire*. At the time, people were talking about the escalation of the Vietnam War, then the escalation of nuclear war. I suggested that the Moscow SALT I agreements between Nixon and Brezhnev were a kind of escalation, and this has been confirmed. What end has the SALT I served? It has promoted the precision of guidance systems, the miniaturization and multiplication of warheads. In other words, thanks to the SALT I agreements concerning arms reduction and limitation, the war-machine has been further sophisticated, and to incredible proportions since the plurality of warheads is further reinforced by their precision. So it seems to me that if they're preparing START agreements on arms reduction, and no longer arms limitation, it's because in reality they foresee an improvement, an even greater sophistication of the war-machine. Agreements between the Americans and the Soviets are agreements on perfecting the war-machine. That is their only purpose, period. And they are allied in this responsibility. There is absolutely no remission for either side. The SALT agreements improved weapons; the START agreements will improve them still further. And they will particularly concern the laser, this is certain. Lasers will soon be operational— already much scientific information confirms this. Now, the laser is a revolution in war politics, since there's no longer a delay—a political delay for decision. There we have something to talk about, in my view.

The coupling of the two imperialisms is an unfriendly understanding. It's deterrence as collusion.

It's deterrence as collusion. The Americans and the Soviets—and the French as well, let's say all the nuclear powers—are involved in this coupled system. It's not by accident that the French left, once in power, voted *unanimously* for an increase in the military budget. For the first time in recent French history. It's significant.

Under these conditions, what is the future of pacifism?

We cannot understand the situation of pacifism today with respect to the dangers of real wars: "The Russians are going to invade Europe, there's going to be a nuclear conflict in the Middle East," etc. It's quite possible that this will happen, but it doesn't interest me in the least.

You don't believe Europe is in a dangerous strategic position?

I believe the notion of geostrategy is being outmoded by the laser and the more sophisticated weapons. The question is no longer about geostrategy, and it's no longer in geopolitics. Sure, there's still the problem of military bases for the forces of intervention and for naval weapons in the Indian Ocean, near the Chinese and Russian territorial boundaries, etc. But we shouldn't confuse bases with geographic politics—with geostrategy. It's a little like saying that parking lots are highways.

The European peace movement as it's developed out of Germany would be out of place in the real problematic.

Yes. The real problematic is Pure War. It's not actual war, but logistical war. So the real problem is to oppose the war-machine as the machine of societal nondevelopment. The problem is not a more-or-less impeding confrontation between the Russians and the Americans, or between blocs. Of course this confrontation could happen, but I would say that this possibility is infinitely smaller, given the speed at which societies—particularly Eastern societies—are exhausted, than the other possibility: endo-colonization.

Isn't the development of pacifist movements on humanitarian grounds a kind of anachronism with respect to the disappearance of man in nuclear armament—instantaneousness, speed, etc.?

The word "pacifist" has meaning (which I adopt) insofar as it is linked to a faith, an official faith confronting another faith. You know that I'm a Christian, and as a Christian I reject nuclear faith because I believe in the peace of Christ. This point of view is of the same nature as the deterrence we were speaking about before. There is undoubtedly in the Polish affair or the German affair (with the Protestant churches) something of a conflict against idolatry. The believer in God protests against the divinity of the ultimate weapon. There they can talk of peace. They can call themselves "pacifists" in the name of a belief which opposes another, idolatrous belief: the missile, no longer the Messiah. It's my point of view, furthermore, but I don't say it's political. I am for the separation of Church and State, I believe combining them would be horrible—it certainly wouldn't spare us any work on politics or transpolitics.

Does working on politics mean questioning technology?

What is happening with technology, what is happening with the war-machine in the heart of industrial society? What is happening with development or nondevelopment, etc.? That should be the real debate. I don't deny the importance of the return of the sacred because, in reality, it was caused by the nuclear age. The nuclear age has put us closer to the apocalypse—this time as the extinction of the species. It's hardly surprising that religious beliefs are unfurling their nags—whether it be Islam, Israel, Jerusalem, "the Eternal City," or the Christian banner. I would say it's perfectly understandable, because facing them is a superb idol they can't accept. I'm a believer, but I'm also political. I believe we need to work on technology, on the essence of technology, as Heidegger said—and thus on the essence of war, that is, the essence of speed. I'll finish with two great phrases by Sun Tsu: "Readiness is the essence of war." What foresight five centuries before Christ. And the second: "Military strength is regulated on its relation to semblance"—everything that has to do with ideologies, hide-and-seek, telecommunications, the impact of audio-visual weapons. That in a nutshell is my account of the present situation. But by answering this way, I give no arms to the militants. Personally, I am not a militant; I couldn't be one. I can only watch and wait.

If the humanitarian perspectives of peace movements are outmoded, then what bases should they build on?

They should try to revive the question of death. Because let's not forget that the gravest danger in post-monarchic society is the concealment of death. In ancient societies, particularly the Greek, the question of death was central. Menander said that for mortals, consciousness is God. We idealize and idolize consciousness because we are mortal. I tend to think we invest inconsciousness, in reason, in history, because we're mortal. A statement like that suggests that if we weren't mortal, there would be no consciousness. If we're conscious, it's because we're mortal. Death and consciousness are allied, thus the consciousness of death is the origin of consciousness. This is important. The entire development of materialism, which is mixed in with industry, exact science, etc., has made us forget that we are mortal. It tends to make us lose consciousness of our status as mortal beings. Marx's statement is interesting: "Consciousness always comes too late." He said it just when dromocracy was developing. I feel like saying, as I did in *L' Esthétique de la disparition*, that in the end, unconsciousness is the aim of Pure War. We are taken by speed. Whence the unconsciousness of the accident, which I find so terrifying. When someone says that we're not interested in accident but in substance, I answer that we're not interested in the death of the object's substance, and thus we are not conscious of that object. Bergson said something that I like very much: "Death is the accident par excellence." And in fact, we are the substance and the accident is death. But this is also true of the technical object. Its accident is the awareness we have of it. If we are not aware of the accident, we are not aware of the object: thus the technological crisis.

To the extent that the accident indeed becomes part of the general economy, death also relies on this economy. If death is not an interruption, and if the interruption is inscribed in life itself, it's with respect to death that we must reconsider life.

Absolutely. Death isn't sad, it's Being itself. Death is the founder of consciousness, and therefore of political awareness.

Isn't death no longer visible because everything is dead? Because we live in civilizations of death?

That would be deterrence. It's the discourse of generalized deterrence: "We're already dead, but we don't know it." All I want to say is simply that political inquiry into death doesn't exist. Even when I read Jean Baudrillard's book *L'échange symbolique et la mort* [The Symbolic Exchange and Death][13]—I'm sorry, but there's not a single warrior in it! So I would say: Let's re-examine our status as mortal beings and we'll again be able to oppose Pure War."

The abolishment of the death penalty is a political answer to the question of death. Do you think this answer gives new life to the question—or does it kill the question once and for all?

When they did away with the death penalty in France six months ago, I felt terrorized. Not that I'm so in favor of capital punishment, but it was the last existing tie between politics and death. Politics (not only in the sense of political thought, but also of administration, the State) is becoming detached from the contemplation of death. The last point on which death still had a relation to politics was capital punishment. Politics conferred death by law. The abolishment of the death penalty, then, was critical insofar as it was simultaneously a means, on the part of the State, of abolishing the question of death. The State, the Ministry of Justice, and the judges decided on death, including its practical execution by the guillotine, hanging, the electric chair, etc. Once capital punishment is abolished, politics ceases to have any relation to death. Finished. Death no longer has any intelligibility. I wasn't hoping for them to keep the death penalty; I was hoping that when they did away with it they would finally begin to question what happens to individual and collective death in a modern society.

Death is displaced, or rather the awareness we can have of it is displaced. As soon as death is hushed up, furthermore, it takes spectacular forms.

Yes; there is transference, due to technology and accident. You see fifteen thousand accident victims on the French highways, more than the toll for the war in Lebanon, and no one thinks twice about it.

At the same time, the death penalty is an anachronism. It's a hold-over from the monarchic order

It's a hold-over from the political awareness of death. If you were a king, or a chief, or a strategist, it's because you had a relation to death which was inscribed within the Law. One was put to death for being a regicide, or one condemned to death (legal dimension). The State-as-destiny, the state of inevitability, means the inevitability of diffused law, and no longer recognized by law.

The Law no longer needs to be written or recognized since it is being made everywhere. It's no longer necessary to incarcerate people, you simply make them disappear. The Law disappears by spreading over everything. And as it's absent, it's always right.

The law is no longer a Law in the political sense: a law which eludes politics is not Law, but mythical law. It's fate. The disappearance of the Law is part of transpolitics.

And yet death returns. Not so much in politics, which is very good at doing without it, but in places to which death has been relegated: hospitals, for example.

Death returns through medicine, through the recent debate on the terminal coma and enforced therapy, on the question of knowing when you can pronounce someone dead. All this is important for inheritances, burial arrangements, etc. And strangely enough, those who are the most active in this matter are the scientists and doctors who wonder if a flat encephalogram is better than a heart that's stopped beating. You remember that woman, Karen Quinlan, who continued to live for five years after they unplugged the machine. There are amazing things about that great interruption which is death.

Which is why philosophers have recently been appointed in some American hospitals to ease the doctors' responsibility. The scientific definition of death by itself is no longer enough. Now you need a moral evaluation as well. In this way the experience of death is reintegrated into social consciousness. We must make the interruption visible and simultaneously attenuate its effects. Kubler-Ross's work on the four stages the dying man must pass through (like the child for Freud!) before reaching resignation is significant. The Law disappears, but it resurfaces elsewhere.

I think it's absolutely scandalous for doctors to be the only ones confronted with the ethical problem of death. Why aren't politicians concerned by it? Why isn't there ever a debate in the National Assembly or a research committee in the Senate to determine what our relation to death will be from now on?

Our relation to death is no longer unified because we now have fragmented bodies. We can make prostheses, perform organ transplants. There are dead parts in the living and living parts in the dead. As there is no longer an identity on the corporal level, and scarcely more on the personal level, isn't it already an insoluble problem?

Yes, but that's why politics no longer exists. Politics was an interpretation of death which differed from the military interpretation. Death is a common experience, the military man fully accepts it; he even builds his career on it, on executioners and victims. The civilian sector confronted the same problematic as the military and reached other conclusions, made other laws, which led to the dichotomy between military and civilian. As soon as the civilian (the political) detaches itself from death, denies it, has nothing more to say about it, we fall body and soul into the militaristic interpretation; we fall under the influence of the military man which then becomes the false priest of the death rite he administers.

Philosophy, or therapy, are there to "clear" the shirking of civil responsibilities.

Yes. The fact that politicians no longer contemplate death immediately discredits them with respect to the military.

You said that it was not the task of politics to analyze death. Then what is it?

The analysis of death is the doctor's work: autopsy, X-rays, encephalograms, heartbeats: the analysis of death on the dissecting table. The politician's task is of another nature, which is linked to the notion of temporality. If we recognize that lived time, time proper, is organized by interruptions, it becomes obvious that death is one of the great organizers of social temporality. It's not by accident that societies were organized by the death rites, the cult of ancestors, etc. The politicians' task, then, is absolutely essential. It consists in saying, today as in the past—but in a different way because of technology—that there are interruptions, including the interruption of death. And it's this interruption of death that we must examine in order to know how to organize it.

Industrial societies have dodged the experience of death. You share some of Georges Bataille's paradoxical positions in this matter. Bataille was in favor of the death penalty because, with death having disappeared from the field of consciousness, we now had to make it reappear We had to make the cut visible, instead of shamefully erecting a pyramid, like in the Place de la Concorde, at the spot where Louis XVI's head fell into a basket.

I am not in favor of the death penalty, I am for death; it's different. For me, death is not negative. Every man is confronted with the great interruption which is death, but society is also confronted with this interruption, in a banal way.

Banal, and panic-stricken at the same time.

Yes, but all the more panic-stricken because we turn our backs on it.

Daniel Cohn-Bendit recently made the shrewd remark that in launching an anti-nuclear campaign, you have to make sure not to frighten people. Capitalist society is already all-too-founded on this fear.

Of course; you have to make sure of that.

The important thing is to make death recognized. We must carefully avoid mobilizing individual anxiety.

Whether there's scientific recognition of death, or whether it's recognition by the philosopher and politician, is all the same to me. We must recognize death. We must recognize it as an organizer, and not as something repressed, something which would lead to a complete impasse, which would serve no end, about which it's better not to speak at all.

For Freud, the death instinct is what governs the organization of great social formations.

The history of religions is no different. That's why I say that the dominical interruption of the Sabbath or Ramadan is an organization of temporality. It's not to worship God: God exists in the organization of time. They don't call it Eternity for nothing. God is what doesn't pass, what isn't inscribed in time. Thus the will to organize time is a questioning of God. Chronopolitics inevitably makes reference to it. Geopolitics came out of the cult of Mother Earth (Alma Mater). The physical relation to Earth was paganism. Chronopolitics is completely different. It's linked to another religious space: a cult of temporality, of immateriality. And that's where you find the question of God—I say *the question*, because there is no answer. This question is just as indelible as the question of death. We cannot, in the name of materialism, say that death doesn't exist, that it's not our problem. To say that God doesn't exist is equally absurd. It's paganism. It's the same as saying that we only hold to that which is good and material, solid, consistent, visible. What an illusion! All the sciences show us that it's not true, that what "is" is not, that I can't believe my eyes. We are in a society that can no longer believe its eyes: that can no longer believe in the reality of matter; than can no longer believe in the reality of physical presence. Holograms show this, make us touch it, so to speak. Science is particularly illuminating on this point: it demystifies matter. And by demystifying matter, it demystifies materialism.

If it's not the role of politics to analyze death, how do you envision approaching the question of death?

Personally, I'm also at odds with this question of death. Why? Because on the one hand I'm a Christian, thus I don't believe in death, but in the soul's immortality; and on the other hand, I don't want to use this faith with respect to those who don't share it. And finally because I don't believe that faith should be an instrument: that would be the worst kind of belief, from which you get the Holy War, religious terrorism, etc. So my return to death is a reflection on disappearance, on the final outcome, on the end, on the fact that what is will cease to exist, on interruption. Whence picnolepsy, little death, etc.… My way of approaching death is both physical and metaphysical. I'm faced here with a problem of writing because I can't hide the fact that I'm a Christian (I don't see why I should hide it, for me it's essential), but on the other hand I don't want to use this "advantage" to challenge things that are common to believers and non-believers alike.

You're saying that the question of God hasn't been raised?

The death of God—I'm speaking of Nietzsche—is an abomination of desolation in recent political history.

The "abomination of desolation"?

It's a biblical term. God isn't dead, it's the question of God that has disappeared in recent history. After Nietzsche, we went from doing away with God to doing away with the question of God, which led to materialism and historical materialism, etc.

But doesn't the question of God return by means of ethnology?

Indeed. It returns through the impact of primitive societies which place death at their centers. And from this point of view I feel closer to rural societies than to my contemporaries. Primitives are at the heart of questions about death, science, politics, and war. Just think of Pierre Clastres. I spent my youth in Breton peasant families where, even though they were Christian, every evening around the fire we discussed myths, great pagan tales, the cart-driver of death: death is a cart that you hear coming, which carries you off. So in some way the vehicle is a vehicle of death, which we also found in Cocteau, with the motorcyclist of Orpheus, for example.

In fact, ours is one of the few societies to have evacuated the question of death. We could even say that one of the major contributions of the Industrial Age was its disappearance.

It's all part of the evacuation of God, since the question of death and the question of God are one and the same. It's "the end." If man were immortal in body and soul, he would be God. And as he isn't immortal, the question of immortality is displaced. Not evacuated, but displaced. And *that* to me is the abomination of desolation. It's sick. My father was a Communist, and although he'd been baptised, like most Italians, he wasn't a believer. But when he died, there was a rift. He was thrown out like garbage, and that I couldn't accept.

Shouldn't we reintroduce the question of God through the question of faith, which includes the beliefs of traditional societies?

The question of God is a large one. The absolute death of nuclear arms, the possibility of suicide open not only to an individual, a society, or even a civilization, but to an entire species, reintroduces the question of God—the question of ethics on another level.

Man has revived the question of God through nuclear accident?

God has come back into history through the door of terror.

12

Pacifism and the Regression
of Politics

The American Pacifist Movement □ Science and the War-Machine □ Peace as War □ Reinventing Life □ Metabolic Speed and Technological Speed □ Sedentariness and De-territorialization □ Marxism and Statistical Thought □ Transpolitics

Let's get back to the pacifist movement. We have seen that it develops a form of resistance which is somewhat displaced with respect to the veritable—logistical—stakes. On the other hand, paradoxically, this movement comes out of Europe which, given the chrono-political dimensions of nuclear arms, is not really on the front line. The development of a peace movement in the United States, in the very heart of the Western scientific-military complex, would certainly be more important, especially if it didn't limit itself to purely moral or humanitarian perspectives, but rather defined a political approach to the scientific war-machine.

That would be an entirely new and promising aspect of resistance. I've always been surprised by the lack of contact, of will to interaction between the European and American peace movements. I personally got in touch with the Archbishop of Seattle, Raymond

G. Hunthausen, who was one of the first, I believe (but this is part of that religious pacifism), to encourage in his parish the non-payment of that part of federal taxes reserved for arms development. There's no doubt that the American "pacifist" militants are at the center of the machine, of the question. They occupy the best position insofar as they also have an extraordinary amount of information on the war-machine at their disposal, which doesn't exist elsewhere—certainly not in France. In France, it's very hard to get new information, whereas in the United States everything is published. Never mind Russia, there isn't any information. Resistance to Pure War can only be based on the latest information.

Furthermore, resistance to Pure War wouldn't be directly affected by events such as in Poland, because the stakes would no longer be ideological.

Absolutely not. Which, moreover, doesn't prevent the existence of several levels within the peace movement itself. I spoke of the level of beliefs, in the general sense. And in fact, I do believe there should be a religious level to show that nuclear power is religious. That's the importance of Holy Wars, of the echo of Holy Wars, for the Christians as well as the Muslims. It reveals the religious nature of deterrence. This level has a future. There is also a more militant and traditional level related to activities of daily resistance, to induced effects or secondary effects of deterrence and its generalization in opposition to police and repression. I'm thinking of the new technique of disappearances which is replacing the Gulags. The disappearance of individuals corresponds to what we were saying on the disappearance of cities. What is the Gulag? It is a kind of anti-city which exists in an invisible territory.

It's still geopolitics.

It's still geopolitics. It's a city—a state of siege, we could say—set up to keep people outside of their traditional relations, or to make them disappear in the case of extermination. The Gulag is still a proof of a society's totalitarian nature. Now, disappearance is a dis-investment. We have nothing to do with it.

It's the disappearance of the place and the individual.

Disappearance of place and individual at the same time. There we have a modernity, a refusal of citizenship, of rights, of habeas corpus, etc. It's now been proven that this technique is spreading all over the world. It's easier to make people disappear one by one, ten by ten, or thousand by thousand than to shut millions up into camps, as they did in Nazi Germany. Even if Gulags and concentration camps still exist—and they do, alas—disappearance is our future.

That's the second level, disappearance as repression.

The third level is what interests me most, but it's not necessarily the most important: the level of opposition to science as a war-machine in itself. To me, the ideology of science as progress is fatal. So there is an analysis of the war-machine in science and technology—tech-nological surprise and scientific surprise—which for me is the essence of resistance. That doesn't mean I'm hoping for an ecological regression, spending our days growing peas, sheep, and roque-fort—no, it means that the other horizon is technical. It's our place, our non-place, if you like. It's what is to be conquered. It's the moon. We must land on the technological continent, and stop believing it's a tool, an instrument for our use, which we can do with as we like.

Technology is not neutral.

It is not neutral; it's a black continent.

A valid peace movement would perhaps, strategically, lean on faith, but simultaneously it should try to reappropriate intelligence.

In other words, reinstitute political intelligence (beyond trans-politics, or the confusion of war-thought and societal thought) through a new knowledge of technology, in the very wide sense.

All ideological or deterrent screens are obstacles to a political understanding of technology; thus, in a certain way, they all contribute to military supremacy.

Absolutely. That's where real deterrence lies. It's in the neutral character (neutral at best—at worst, benevolent) of scientific and technical development. I believe that here we have an extraordinary unknown quantity, which must be unmasked or uncovered. The pacifists of the 1930s opposed real war, a war inscribed in its practical execution. Pacifists today oppose the tendency toward war, in other words the war for preparation for war. Not a hypothetical war which could begin in France, China, or elsewhere, but war as scientific and technological preparation.

They oppose peace as war.

They oppose peace as war, as infinite preparation which exhausts and will eventually eliminate societies. In any case, the apocalypse is here. It could happen at any moment, but the interesting argument is that apocalypse is hidden in development itself, in the development of arms—that is, in the nondevelopment of society.

From a civilization of death, we would have to reinvent life.

Absolutely. Politics in the ancient sense of the Greek *polis*, the Greek city, has never been anything else. It was an enormous invention. They extracted life from death, from the relation to death, from the awareness of death. They extracted a life which had its own status: citizenship; which had its own ideology, its own culture, its own knowledge: philosophy. From the barbarity of ancient times, they extracted, not a way of life (as they say nowadays), but a life proper. A life with character. We could say that politics *consecrated* life, in the religious sense. That's what the role of politics is. Giving money to the poor or taking money from the rich is all secondary, tricks of the trade. The real problem is: what kind of life? I saw some graffiti on the walls of Belfast this summer which said, "Is there life before death?" It struck me because it's completely tied in with the age of deterrence: deterrence tends to deny the existence of life before death. No need to die, we're already the living dead.

Politically speaking, strategically speaking, how could we reinvent life?

The question of death and the question of life are enormous philosophical problems. Life is generally identified with a biographical duration, a history—but a microhistory, that of an individual from birth to death. It's an historicistic view of life. Can we imagine life otherwise? Isn't life also a matter of intensity? That's the problem. Is the problem to live to be eighty, or is it to live until forty—but live intensely? I don't mean intensity as we were using it before. I mean something you can experiment with. What does it mean to live a day intensely? I would say it's to put your finger on relativity. A day can last a thousand years, and a thousand years can last a day. There's a relation of intensiveness that hasn't been politicized yet. Life has been linked to its duration, its slow development, its proliferation in generation, children, wealth, accumulation of inheritance, heirs, territory—in other words, an extensive dimension. Can't we envision, isn't it encumbent upon us to imagine what an intensive life would be? Being alive means to be lively, quick. Being lively means being-speed, being-quickness. Being-liveliness. All these terms challenge us. There is a struggle, which I tried to bring to light, between metabolic speed, the speed of the living, and technological speed, the speed of death which already exists in cars, telephones, the media, missiles. There is also a couple formed by the metabolic speed of the living and the technological speed of deterrence. Politics should try to analyze this interface, because without this analysis a fatal coupling will be established, as I tried to demonstrate in *L'esthétique de la disparition*, particularly with video, subliminal effects, etc., which take consciousness "by speed." Video is a weapon that takes over consciousness itself. After glasses, after hearing aids, we have a kind of prosthesis for the liveliness of consciousness. It's strange that the concept of speed was omitted in the development of knowledge. If we consider the history of humanity from the point of view of speed—of both metabolic and technological speed—it sheds new light on the development of societies which can help us analyze past societies, as well as our own—our own as non-society, as society in non-becoming.

The stakes have now become universal, and yet we still function simultaneously on a geopolitical level: Germany, Europe, the revival of peace movements in the United States.... How can we reconcile the relatively traditional forms of political intervention with the emergency state of a technological civilization rushing toward its own death?

In each lived period, there are overlappings of different ages. We know that at this very moment we are living in both the Neolithic Age (in the depths of Amazonia or with the Australian aborigines) and the Nuclear Age. What I've just said doesn't dismiss all that with a wave of the hand. There are very differentiated coexistences in this world between "primitive" ways of life, "classical" ways of life, and finally "futuristic" ways of life. I'm not trying to deny that all this coexists. When I speak, what I say always has a somewhat absolute side; I unintentionally identify with what I'm denouncing. What seems central to me is the question of place. In some way, place is challenged. Ancient societies were built by distributing territory. Whether on the family scale, the group scale, the tribal scale, or the national scale, memory was the earth; inheritance was the earth. The foundation of politics was the inscription of laws, not only on tables, but in the formation of a region, nation or city. And I believe this is what is now challenged, contradicted by technology. None of the so-called great politicians today are able to approach the kind of modernity we've tried to talk about here. None. All of them have arguments, a "sales pitch" that dates from the nineteenth century. Their problem is still territorialized inscription, in other words the negation of the technical fact. Now, technology—Gilles Deleuze said it—is deterritorialization. It's no accident that my first book (I hadn't read Deleuze at the time) was called *L'insécurité du Territoire*. Deterritorialization is the question for the end of this century.

So then, what succeeds the inscription of laws, duties, and statutes in a place? Can politics find new foundations in this absolute nomadism that forms the technical horizon? What forms could political intervention take in the context of absolute deterritorialization?

I believe the question of sedentariness and our relation to intensity is central. I began to ask that question in "Revolutionary Resistance," the second chapter of *Popular Defense and Ecological Struggles*. That's where the question of politics lies, if politics has a future.

Which isn't sure?

Which isn't sure. But if politics has no future, it's the end. It means the State will have exhausted the world (the State in the sense of absolute State, pure State founded on the ultimate weapon, the divinity of the nuclear arm, etc.).

At least, at this point, politics no longer passes through ideology.

For me, no, certainly not. It's hard to pinpoint for the moment. We are facing a situation which is so apocalyptic, which so surpasses and exceeds limits and formations…. What we were saying before about the end of territorial formations is true of all formations, including our discourse. We cannot proceed in very rigorous fashion. We can barely show tendencies. In the 1950s, Churchill said, "In ancient warfare, the episodes were more important than the tendencies; in modern warfare, the tendencies are more important than the episodes." In other words, we are confronted no longer with episodes—the Vietnam War, the Polish affair, the

Egyptian-Israeli conflict, etc.—but with tendencies, a statistical vision of the world in which we are inscribed by technology, by the movement of science and technology. And it's not easy to grasp statistical perspectives. Knowing that the Russians crossed the Oder and throwing it back in their faces is very clear. But a tendency—how do you recognize a tendency? Already it's said that no one's ever met a social class. Malraux said that statistical thought is more important than Marxism. The influence of statistics on contemporary thought hasn't been measured yet: I'm thinking of Vauban, the great logistics expert and statistician, the great fortress expert—still another military figure.

There is at least one sure thing: that politics now passes through nuclear power.

Yes. Through the military, in other words nuclear power, because the military *is* nuclear power. There is no civilian nuclear power. It's obvious. For many, "transpolitics" was a vision à la Baudrillard—moreover, that's how he understands it: a relatively positive vision. For me, it is totally negative. It's the contamination of traditional political thought by military thought, period! There is nothing positive in my use of the term transpolitics. It's not post-politics, it's not the end of politics, it is its contamination. It's completely negative. Transpolitics means no more politics at all.

13

The North-South Inversion

The End of the East-West Axis □ The Elimination of Europe □
A New Yalta □ The Gateway to the Sea □ Budapest, Prague,
Poland □ Walesa and the Pope □ The Priest vs. the Warrior □
Holy Non-War □ Vatican II and Deterrence □ Internal Collapse □
German and Polish Pacifists □ Solidarity □ Death as Weapon □
Decline of an Empire □ Paradox of Soviet Nondevelopment □
Humanism and Religion

*How do you see the current world situation? Are new tendencies
developing in the strategy of the major powers?*

The East-West axis is now tipping toward the North-South axis.
Simply realize that it was the Soviet army that put down the Hun-
garian uprising; that the Warsaw Pact suppressed springtime in
Prague; that the Polish army suppressed Polish trade unionism.
Whereas it was the Soviet army that invaded Afghanistan. Thus we
can see a withdrawal of the East-West situation, a strategic toppling
which means that they now leave the armies of satellite countries
the responsibility of dealing with internal unrest. Lenin said that
"strategy is the choice of where to apply force." The Soviets'

choice of where to apply force is obviously North-South, toward the Persian Gulf, Afghanistan, and China. It's another axis. From this point of view, I'm not worried about a threat to Europe. I don't believe Europe is threatened by the Soviet Union. On the other hand, I believe North-South thrusts are the way of the future.

Are these thrusts converted into energy? The Persian Gulf is the oil road, after all.

Of course there's the aspect of the energy flow in the Persian Gulf, but there's also a reversal of the tendency. Every strategy follows a line of thrust. If we study military history, we realize that since the beginning, practically, since the fighting kingdoms of China, there has been an extraordinary constancy in the line of thrust, which has always been East-West. Furthermore, it's been the path of the great emigrations. Now, it seems that since the advent of deterrence, there has been a North-South inversion, of which Afghanistan is a sign, as was Vietnam. That's where power relations are still located, where future conflicts will be. Not only to cut off the oil road, but also because there has been an inversion of the positions of the lines of force—with respect to supply lines as well as to planetary tensions, as we saw with the Falklands.

American opposition to the invasion of Afghanistan was much stronger and the pressure much more constant than for Poland.

Afghanistan is for the Soviet Union what the Falklands were for England and America. Europe is entirely out of the running here.

And first of all because it decolonized Africa: it's obvious that European colonization was situated, albeit in a different way, along the North-South axis.

So you don't believe we can hope to see a third "bloc" form around Europe. Is the elimination of Europe as a political power now an established fact?

Absolutely. Europe will be identified with the Third World.

Do you think we'll see a new division of the world—the negotiation of a new Yalta?

Yalta 1 will give rise—and this has already begun—to a Yalta 2. The SALT talks were only its preamble. There will probably be a depolarization of Americans and Soviets which will not be to Europe's benefit. China's influence will obviously be considerable here.

In fact, China has been conspicuously absent from our interview.

We can't talk about everything.

China is located right on the North-South axis.

The tension between China and the Soviet Union is infinitely greater than between the Soviet Union and Europe. Afghanistan and Vietnam are examples.

China is a big piece of territory.

Yes, but it's also the access to the sea. The problem of naval power has become a major one with deterrence. Already the European colonial empire was favored by the naval might of England and France. But it's obvious that with nuclear power and the deterritorialization we were speaking of, nations with large coastal regions are highly coveted. No wonder there are struggles for possession of the islands: mercenaries in the Seychelles, socialists on Mauritius.

Isn't geostrategy totally disqualified by the existence of nuclear submarines and satellites?

What's disqualified is the surface area. The liquid or solid surface is disqualified in favor of submarines and satellites. What's still important is under the sea, underground, or in space. Every visible power is threatened.

Disappearance is our future....

From now on power is in disappearance: under the sea with nuclear submarines, in the air with U-2's, spy-planes, or still higher with satellites and the space shuttle, in its first military voyage—voyage from North to South, but also from Zenith to Nadir.

We've talked a lot about Europe and the United States, but very little about the USSR. I'd like to begin extending our analysis to this other element of the fatal couple by discussing the Polish affair.

In November 1980, I was having dinner with my friend Nanni Balestrini and a journalist from *La Stampa* who had just come back from Warsaw and wanted to ask me about the war. He told me what had happened in Poland. It was the end of Kania; Jaruzelski hadn't been nominated yet. He asked me what I thought of the situation. I told him there was no doubt that the Polish army was going to intervene. And this journalist, a specialist on Poland, who speaks the language, said: "That doesn't hold water." Several months later Jaruzelski was appointed, and a year after that it was indeed the Polish army that intervened. How had I been able to predict that? It wasn't prophecy, it was the movement of endo-colonization in the great empires being confirmed. The situation in Latin America is completely symmetrical to the Balkan one. What happened in Budapest? In Budapest it was the Russians who stepped in, no problem. They took the KGB out of their political commissariats and shot them. What happened in Prague? Of course the Soviets lent a hand for taking the control tower in Prague, but it was really the Warsaw Pact that intervened. Thus it was completely logical in the doctrine of endo-colonization, of endo-repression, that this time the so-called "popular" army of a popular democracy itself act as the police. The situation of the Soviet empire works on this self-repression—which furthermore is a phase of every submission. You begin by exercising constraints by means of force. Only look at what they've done with pets. First animals were put in cages, then domesticated, in the sense that they were taught certain tricks and customs. Then they were led to mutate biologically. We see the same thing in imperialism. External repression, control over populations by external forces, is progressively superseded by a "mediatization" of this repression, and finally by a very clear, very banal self-repression. That's what happened in Poland. The only novelty is that it happened on the side of Polish trade unionism.

Do you see a relation between the German peace movement and the emergence of Polish trade unionism?

For me, trade unionism is a form of civil war. Anarchistic trade unionism used the strike as a means of combat; it's a military structure. Basically, the union is a combat commando against management. The interesting thing in the Polish affair is that there's a coupling of trade unionism and religious belief. There is no Walesa without the Pope; there's no Polish affair without Walesa. The union doesn't have the power to dominate the party without invoking religious faith. That's what makes Walesa powerful. The only difference in the new tripartition constituted by Jaruzeiski the warrior, Glemp the priest, and Walesa the worker is that this time it's the priest who confronts the warrior. For in reality, Walesa is the priest's man. He's not so much a union leader as a man of faith recognized by the Pope. Glemp-Walesa form a couple and the warrior, Jaruzelski, stands alone. Thus, the conflict is between two supremacies: an imperialistic and military supremacy (Jaruzelski's) and an imperialism in the cosmic or mythical sense, which is Catholicism. If we look at recent events, the fall of Lebanon, the fall of Iran—how is it that hyper-powerful armies such as Iran's, or at least solid ones such as Lebanon's, could suddenly fall, with almost no resistance? Because they crumbled precisely from within, because of a religious conflict. Now, I believe that here and there are both the same. What is interesting in Poland, within Christianity (to use a term which, moreover, is outmoded, like all institutions) with respect to Islam, is that Khomeini opted for a traditional Holy War—Mullahs preaching with rifles—whereas Walesa and Glemp called for Holy Non-War. They could very well have said that since strikes no longer worked, they would take up

arms. Nothing of the kind: they said, "No, we will not fight, we will not be terrorists." And that's really something: it would suggest that Christian ecumenicalism is a kind of answer to deterrence. It's a deterrence from religious conflict. Ecumenicalism was a way of making peace between the three great monotheisms, and even beyond, since there are research committees on animism in Africa. Perhaps we haven't analyzed Vatican II very well. Vatican II appeared at a time when strategies of deterrence were beginning in Russia and in Europe. Thus, in my opinion, the Polish affair is especially original in the importance it gives the religious question with respect to the military question. And the same for the future of the Soviet problem: what's happening with the religious question in the Soviet Union? Because the only way to "liquidate" the Soviet statocracy—the military class—is from within. Not by a mass uprising against the technocrats, the weapons factories, the "nomenclaturists" of the Soviet war, but an internal collapse similar to what's begun to happen in Poland. And that would be supremely dangerous for the Soviet empire. That's why, in a certain sense, I don't really see the difference between the German and Polish pacifists. For me they're pacifists as soon as they've renounced terrorism, including in a state of war. They've refused to bear arms. Walesa is a pacifist. He wants to conquer by the strike, not by the shotgun.

You said that the strike was also a weapon.

Of course it's a weapon, but do you see what I mean? Walesa doesn't want to regress with respect to the situation he himself has imposed. In some ways, the Poles are in the same boat as the German pacifists. They, too, have a heavy cross to bear. If on the one hand

the Poles "support" Soviet imperialism, on the other the young Germans, our friends, have to bear the immense burden of Naziism, which is still part of their make-up.

But trade unionism à la Walesa is not trade unionism as it developed in Europe, as management of society. There's been a transformation of unionism—and of the proletariat along with it—from weapon of combat into weapon of conciliation, not to say cooperation.

Solidarity-style trade unionism is hardly trade unionism at all. That's why it went out of control. The Polish trade unionists set themselves up as a counter-power. From the outset, as pacifists, they sought to establish a dialogue with the politicians. And when they'd gotten the maximum out of the State, they tried the army indirectly, of course. When Jaruzelski came to power, Walesa said: "We love our military, we're ready to talk with them." The only thing I've never understood, but which was certainly in the air, is why they didn't propose Solidarity in the armed forces.

There was a hint of something in this direction with the national alliance, the fireman's academy.

I imagine something of that order was played out in the national alliance meeting between Jaruzelski, Walesa, and Glemp. But contrary to Kania, the army refused the "non-party" dialogue. (The Portuguese used to say, "We are a non-party revolution.") Solidarity did the same. It bypassed the Party from the moment the Party began to dissolve. The Party was bypassed because it was collapsing, because it no longer had any supporters. Solidarity questioned the army, but the army refused to answer. At that

point, the leaders of Solidarity bluntly proposed to go get the Russians. "We've got ten million supporters," they said, "we don't want to take up arms, we don't want war, so we'll talk with the Russians—we'll talk with anybody." They're Christians, don't forget. They have an essential weapon, the Great Beyond. Still the problem of relation to death. What gives Holy War its absolute power? It's *not fearing* death. It's the fact that history doesn't stop with the last beep on the encephalograph. "So we'll go talk with the Russians; we'll talk with the Devil if we have to." They were ready to go to extremes, which was the only way to topple the army. For the moment, at least, I can't see any other way. To liquidate the absolute power of the armies, whether under the Warsaw Pact or NATO, I see no other alternative at this time than by making an appeal to faith. By raising the question of death again, in other words by reexamining politics. What more can politics bring to the question of death than religion? It's an ancient question which is constantly raised with each new social and political formation. It's the relation to death that determines whether or not we exist. In this sense, Walesa is very close to the German pacifists. What did Walesa say? He said: "We're already dead in Eastern Europe. Our nationalities are already extinct. We exist in decline, our life is a non-life, so we have nothing to lose by confronting the enemy, whether it be the Russians, the military, etc." Moreover, he was strengthened by the words of the French bishops who said: "If suicide is forbidden to the individual, it is even more forbidden to a nation: a nation has no right to commit suicide." For the individual, it's a point that can be argued, since they're already debating the right to suicide. But for a State, a nation—never! I would rephrase this by asking whether a species has an even greater right to commit suicide. And here's where we come back to the German pacifists. So on the one hand there is a nation, Poland, which refuses suicide, which considers itself already dead, but which doesn't want to prolong its own death and self-torture indefinitely. Hence Walesa. On the other hand, there are the Germans who have experimented with— who practically invented—Total War, and who say, "We won't accept nuclear suicide." Things become clearer. It's all very political, you see, but in the ancient sense. I can't say it any better than that.

That's an analysis of the Polish situation in an endo-political perspective. But Poland is also a symptom of Russia. The shortages in Poland are really those of the Soviet empire.

If you reread the first chapters of *L'insécurité du Territoire*, which were written in 1969, I already said what Hélene Carrere d'Encausse, a Soviet specialist, carefully documented in *Decline of an Empire*[14]: every empire is threatened. The Soviet Union is an empire which perhaps hasn't exploded, but which is breaking apart. Which furthermore is what happened to the American empire. It's no longer a formed empire, but a cultural one; more the empire of a way of life than of territory. Truly immediatized. I believe the Soviet Union is an empire watching its geographical status break down little by little, from Islam on the Southern border to Eastern Europe on the Western border.

The East German playwright Heiner Müller feels that the future holds the internal erosion of both blocs, in other words the appearance of the Third World within both the USSR and the United States.[15]

That's endo-colonization and nondevelopment. There are no more developing societies, but only societies tending toward nondevelopment, or underdevelopment in the civilian sector. It's obvious that Latin America or Africa are a prefiguration of what will happen within the great blocs. It's certain, and it won't begin in Europe. After Africa and Latin America, which are what they are, we have the Soviet Union which simply decided not to develop. That's what's new about the Soviet Union. It's got a head start on Total Peace, because it hasn't developed consumption. So we can say that what is advanced about the Soviet Union is that it's an imperialist power which already practices at home what others practice outside their own boundaries. The post-Khrushchev period saw the refusal to keep up with the American way of life: the refusal to develop.

In other words, the Soviets took a short cut.

And taking short cuts gave them a certain advantage on the level of military investment.

Paradoxically, it was by maintaining in itself underdevelopments of the African and South American type that the Soviets have gained a head start over consumer societies.

All of '68 was against the consumer society. All the youth and student movements (there are many names for them) at the end of the '60s in the West were, to my mind, signs of the danger of gluttonous consumption. The exaggeration of consumption was pointing toward something fearsome, even though it remained diffused. Not that the students themselves (most of whom were middle class) had been against a relative development of consumption: but they understood that its excesses were leading toward collapse. In this consumption beyond all limits, there was a prefiguration of collapse and of Western civilian society's nondevelopment.

Another paradox is that the nondevelopment of consumption in the USSR makes it dependent on the United States. In some ways, there is a division of labor between the two warring blocs.

It reinforces the couple. There's a large debate on whether a society is defined by consumption, or whether consumption is the hidden phase of the means of destruction.

Extravagant consumption. Western-style potlatch.

Personally, having shown what happens between military and civilian consumption, I don't believe we can define a politics that way. It's another echo of the illusion of progress from the Industrial Revolution, the illusion of Darwinian evolution, etc. I don't believe we should forbid consumption: we've seen that it's the tendency, in any case. But that's not really the level at which we can analyze. It's not central, it's secondary. I don't claim to define the situation. I try to reveal tendencies. And I think I've revealed a number of important ones: the question of speed; speed as the essence of war; technology as producer of speed; war as logistics, not strategy; war as preparation of means and no longer as battles, declaration of hostilities. Endo-colonization: the colony has always been the model of the political State, which began in the city, spread to the nation, across the communes, and reached the stage of the French and English colonial empires. And now it backfires, which we knew the moment there was decolonization. Decolonization is not a positive sign, it's an endo-colonial sign. If you decolonize without, you'll colonize all the more intensely within. Colonial extensiveness is replaced by endo-colonial intensiveness.

And intensiveness corresponds to instantaneousness.

It corresponds to instantaneousness, the end of history as biographical narrative of societies, peoples, nations, and cultures.

And the end of man.

Yes, the end of man as humanism. Whence the return of the religious question. Because for me, the religious question is not internal to humanism, but external. It's a question, not the answer. The question of religion lies outside of humanism.

14

The Fatal Couple and

the Supreme Idol

Mutual Simulation of the Two "Blocs" □ Vietnam and Watergate □ Internal Collapse of Communism □ Backwash of Marxist Ideology □ The End of the Straits □ The Falklands and Antarctica □ Dematerialization of Physical Space □ Absolute Unity □ The Exterminating Opposition □ Pure War

Let's talk more in detail about the USSR, the other member of the fatal couple. To favor American imperialism—or Soviet imperialism, as Castoriadis recently did—is to uncouple the nuclear phenomenon, and thus to "de-deter" it.

We don't know much about the USSR. Information is scarce, and thus the image we can have of this country is pretty uncertain. There is a radical gap between our way of envisioning politics and society, and what happens in the Soviet Union. I would have nothing to say about it on the strictly political level, except—coming back to biography—that my father was a Communist and worshiped Stalin. Needless to say that for me, Communism on the level of political philosophy has always been something awful. So let's forget about social life and talk about the geostrategic existence of the USSR. With military thought, things become much simpler. I'm thinking of Clausewitz's phrase: "In war everything is simple, but simplicity is difficult."

Coupling is simplicity itself. It's at the root of all conflict.

You're right to say that the USSR and the United States are coupled. When you talk about the Soviet Union, you have to talk about the United States, and vice-versa. Together they form a system. The American military-industrial complex was the model for the Soviet military-industrial complex. The Soviets were fascinated by the Americans. You hear more and more that they've now surpassed them: sure, it's not the quantity that counts, it's the quality. Because strategy is more qualitative than quantitative—in nuclear power, that is, in mass power. The Soviet Union is America's former student, a student which has free reign in matters of war economy since in a socialist economy you can invest capital any way you want. This said, the Soviet military-industrial complex, the "stratocracy," as Castoriadis says, is only an image, a reflection of the American military class. So we can't understand the evolution of the Soviet Union on the geostrategic and military levels without looking at what's happening in America. We know that real power in the United States is in the hands of the Pentagon. The American military class passed the buck of the Vietnam failure to the political class, which happened to be Nixon. Watergate was a magic trick which allowed the American military class to come out safe and sound by discrediting politics.

It's not so simple, for bouncing Nixon simultaneously allowed them to whitewash the political class and democratic institutions.

If they hadn't bounced Nixon, it would have been the United States' first military defeat. The American army didn't want to accept responsibility for this defeat. The recognition of defeat is something we know in France and in Europe—not so in the United States. If the American army had taken responsibility for this defeat, it would have induced extraordinary effects, unheard-of political backfire. Just look at Argentina. I can imagine these effects, but they were repressed. Watergate occurred at just the right time, putting the President in the limelight—and not the strategists, the generals, the war-machine. But just as Watergate showed the tensions that existed all the same (even in a country like the United States) between the political and military classes, the same thing is occurring in the Soviet Union. It's less visible, but still, when Brezhnev appointed himself Field Marshall several years ago, I found it very interesting. It meant going into the military ritual when there was no need to. That surprised me. People thought it was a trick, an old man who wanted to be decorated. I think it was more serious. Since the second nuclear revolution, since the creation of intercontinental missiles, the military class has been acquiring power in the Soviet Union. Not only with respect to the State apparatus and war economy, but also with respect to the political apparatus itself. So it's sure that the more time passes, and the more technologies develop, the more powerful the Soviet army becomes—and the more Communism becomes a facade, a banner—which someday, most likely, will no longer even be necessary. The internal elimination of Communism in East-West power relations is what's in store.

By the same token, Star Wars takes on the dimensions of a political manifesto: you have the Good Guys versus the Bad Guys, or the Greens versus the Reds. Furthermore, it was in these Manichean terms that Reagan defined the conflict of the two classes.

Yes, and that's why I no longer believe the current situation is a situation of ideological war. When you say East and West, it's already a dual function between two different forms of empire, and especially between two empires of which one is the other's student. The Soviet Empire in its industrial and military form is an avid student of the American Empire's military might. We have to treat them together. We can't understand one without the other. As for the question of Communism's subversive value, I think it's completely outmoded. Moreover, China is a good example. The shockwave of Communism was Marx's England, the French Commune, the Spartacists, the Russian Revolution, then China, Vietnam—only to smother in the African continent. Then there's the backwash: the end of Maoism, the decline of the satellite countries and socialist republics, in anticipation of the decline of Socialist states in Africa and elsewhere. There's an enormous back-wash of Marxist ideology in its power to mobilize. But I believe this refusal is the consequence of a development of knowledge about war and power relations, which no longer has anything to do with the masses and collectives forming the basis of Socialism. Socialism is the dictatorship of the proletariat. Once you've abandoned the dictatorship of the proletariat, you've abandoned Communism.

So Pure War corresponds to pure confrontation.

Pure, technical, technocratic confrontation, of which the Americans are the absolute symbol, the Soviets being only their emulators.

The problem now is to know which of the two political regimes is more apt to set up an effective war-machine. The nondevelopment of Russian civilian society, which gives the military free reign, could itself become a model for the Americans.

Of course it's a model. If the Russians were inspired by American military development for their war-machine, the Americans tend to be or will be inspired—as we're starting to see with Reagan—by Soviet nondevelopment to do the same thing at home. Moreover, it's what they have started to do in South America. There's a phenomenon of mutual simulation.

How has the North-South inversion affected this phenomenon of reciprocal simulation?

All geostrategic organization was founded on an East-West orientation. The great traditional Indo-European emigration flows went in this direction. All the obligatory places of passage were hotbeds of subversion in the political sense, and of domination in the military sense. It was just as much the Balkans, the Dardanelles, the Bosporus, as the Mediterranean, Egypt, the Suez Canal, and Gibraltar with what's happening around it. You had an entire East-West confrontation. Now, there is an absolute North-South inversion. By North-South, I don't mean following a developed country/ underdeveloped country axis, but strictly in geographic terms. The Falklands war showed it. It's the end of narrow passes, of the importance of passages, straits, isthmuses. It began with the Suez campaign, which was still an East-West war. The Suez War brought about an extraordinary transformation in containers and ships that passed by Cape Horn. There was an inversion: flows no longer passed through the little canals—Suez, Panama, Gibraltar, or the Bosporus—but into the open sea: Cape Horn, Cape of Good Hope, the Indian Ocean, and of course South Africa and Antarctica. This inversion is related to the arteries of the Persian Gulf and the passage of the great oil channels. But it's more than that: It's the entire East-West conflict tipping toward the North-South axis. Power becomes a function of deterrence. It's no longer simply a matter of quantitative might—the number of warships afloat, the Home Fleet—it's also the nuclear submarines on which deterrence rests. We saw it with the START agreements. The Americans proposed reducing ground forces by half, since the Russians get their power from ground forces and the Americans from nuclear submarines. The Americans played the card of naval power—still qualitative—the submarine being their trump card. A nuclear submarine passing Suez or Panama, however, is no longer really deterrent. It's not really deterrent except when on the open sea. So this disqualification affects all arms systems, all power relations. They realize that they can only play on the Southern passageways. From this point on, the Persian Gulf/Indian Ocean passage leads up toward the Atlantic, the North Atlantic/South Atlantic, and Pacific passageway. And here the Antarctic becomes a crucial geostrategic pole. It's not by chance that everyone got so involved in the Falklands war. Some say the conflict was over oil—that wasn't the question. The question was that there was a new geostrategic situation and that the Antarctic would be its center, its axis. Once the North-South axis takes prevalence on the geostrategic level, we notice that the struggle between the Soviet Union and the United States is no longer the same. The fate of America, Latin America, and Europe is no longer the same. No wonder America isn't being generous with Europe at the moment. There is an inversion, a tipping which is worth analyzing, which is linked to both the submarines' freedom of movement and the great oil flows which no longer pass by straits and canals.

The two empires are risking internal disintegration, but eternally there seems to be a process of mutual justification, a reciprocal geostrategic reinforcement which bodes ill for the future.

The Russian-American coupling began as opposition, and it's slowly becoming, with technical progress and the reduction of the world to nothing, a conspiracy. I once joked that we would perhaps see a take-over by the Soviet and American military class, and that at bottom they could very well grab power together. A take-over on the scale of the Pure State. I even worked out a whole situation, saying their capital would probably be in Switzerland....

At the same time, it would mean negating the motivation for war. That's all political fiction; but what we have in reality is a struggle which is all the more irrepressible in that the conflict runs in idle.

A struggle means to organize, master, produce a space-time. If there are geostrategic inversions, it's because there are still ancient situations, because we still haven't reached chrono-political nirvana, because there's still space somewhere, and this space still imposes a few constraints (but fewer and fewer)—since passage by Cape Horn and Latin America is still a deterritorialization. The fact that naval power and orbital weapons are absolute power shows quite well that physical space is dematerializing and losing more and more of its importance.

Ideologies are also dematerializing. The motivations for conflict are becoming less and less credible, or acceptable. Pure War is a conflict which has virtually none of the objectives traditionally ascribed to war. Paradoxically, this makes it all the harder to master.

The abandonment of ideological war came out of technical development. Technology offers destructive capabilities too great for war to still be limited to the acquisition of territory, influence, wealth, or subjects. Ideological war has become Holy War. The technical surprise destroys the aims of war—and eventually war itself, the motivation for war—in favor of its infinite preparation. The necessity of war is no longer in its execution, but in its preparation. Its preparation is economic war. Given that the war-machine is being developed more and more without ever being used, without anyone even thinking of using it (remember the surprise about the Exocet, which is already an old machine), it's obvious that the destructive effect has passed into the economy, into the nondevelopment of civilian society.

The conflict's ideological aspect serves more and more as a smokescreen for a pure conflict of national interests. Although it's condemned the European states for their participation in building the Siberian pipeline, the United States hasn't stopped shipping grain to the USSR. So we can wonder what's still at stake? What is the real motivation for the conflict when ideologies are disintegrating to leave room for the superpowers' cynicism? You spoke of examining death. What do we examine now? Power? War? The conflict itself?

We must examine unity—and that's where the question of God reappears. What exists in the tension between Russia and America is the desire for unity, for the world to be one. Of course it's not said; it's not explicit or expressible. But I think it's the realization of an absolute State, of a single earth. The tension began with Alexander the Great and continues between the two great powers.

Is this comparable to the great invasions? Is it a return of the Huns?

No: that was the ancient phase. Now it's no longer in the realm of invasion, but in the realm of conformity: that the world becomes one, that it has a single form, and that I can identify with it.

It's the mythic projection of war.

Absolute unity is what deterrence aims toward. Deterrence has begun to realize this Pure State.

But it's a unity which works by division. If there weren't two blocs, there would be no conflict. As William Burroughs suggested, if we implanted electrodes directly into the brain and could control it absolutely, there would be nothing left to control. Wouldn't this be the very limit of all present conflict: that we must now maintain political motivations, preserve ideological pertinence and a certain amount of national independence at all costs, more and more artificially—or else the conflict will disappear?

That's a large question. The only answer we can still give is that there is a tendency toward unity—but an exterminating unity, one which is accomplished precisely in nondevelopment.

Geostrategy goes hand in hand with a process of domestic exploitation; the conflict is transferred to the heart of civilian society. The tendency toward unity showing through the increasingly empty and irreducible conflict of the two blocs overlaps the emergence of a new despotism.

It's obvious that the opposition is less real between the American and Soviet armies than between the American military class and its central or outlying populations—the latter being Latin America and Europe. Where do we find battle against an external adversary? There is none.

But exactly where is the internal adversary? The military class, after all, can hardly be distinguished from the civilian population if we consider the entire scientific and industrial complex a crystallization of the military. Doesn't denouncing the military class' hold over its own population finally come down to artificially maintaining oppositions just where they're beginning to blur?

No, I don't think so. Depletion is quite real; Reagan's plan for reorganization is quite real; endo-colonization is a working phenomenon, and it's quite real: it's an exterminating opposition. That's the suicide State: the two powers have constituted their opposition in the name of History, and on the daily level they only think about their own populations, about emptying out their own underground, if you like.

But the military class exhausts itself in technological advance which it made its spearhead and the driving force of its domination. From now on decision is becoming more and more dependent on pure technology.

I agree. The military class doesn't worry about the technocratic dimension. It pursues its advantage without realizing that the men composing it will be eliminated just the way they're getting rid of the working class they no longer need, since they can get the work done by some poor slob in Hong Kong. That's why I'm not anti-militaristic, but worse. That's why I always distinguish between the military class, the men composing it, and its means. These men are also headed for extinction within the military apparatus. Remember what Commander Salt of the "Sheffield" said about that devastating missile attack: "It's staggering. It's a new kind of war, unknown to experts." This last sentence perfectly illustrates the present revolution in modes of destruction. The doctrine of production has replaced the doctrine of use on the battlefield. The computer already has the last word. If the use of weapons is no longer taught at the Military Academy, it's because the time for decision is now insufficient. We no longer need the man of war, just as we no longer need the proletarian who was also a man of war, a man of industrial war in the large steel industries of the past where they worked on the assembly line. The progressive elimination (which is already quite advanced) of the proletariat in the industrial machine runs parallel with the elimination of individuals in the war-machine.

So it's not only the state which is suicidal; the war-machine is also self-destructing.

The suicide State is a state committing suicide, and everything gets caught in it! The tragic thing about the technocrats is that they never ask themselves that question. Never! The captain of a French nuclear submarine recently said, "Once I've fired my volley, I'll commit suicide in my submarine." That's really a man of war's statement: I kill them and then myself. It's kamikaze. It's just the opposite of politics. The politician says: "We'll see. Before firing the volley, we'll talk it over." The crews of nuclear submarines are not appointed, they're all volunteers. The captain doesn't ask himself the question, or rather he asks it and negates it at the same time by saying, "Firing the volley is so serious that I'll commit suicide afterward." He would do well to think of suicide beforehand! He should ask about suicide now, not afterward, instead of freely becoming the captain of a nuclear submarine which is a suicide State unto itself. That's where the warrior is a false priest. The priest speaks before death, he talks about the afterlife before death. He is still in the realm of politics. That's why there are very tight bonds between religion and politics.

The military class' hegemony over the civilian population is therefore illusory, in the long run. The two values are not only opposed: by opposing each other, they implode.

Pure War no longer needs men, and that's why it's pure. It doesn't need the human war-machine, mobilized human forces. It was hardly a generation ago that we stopped needing assembled masses to provide an abundance, as Bernanos said of the troops in World War I who went to attack Verdun: "That troop of extras has been gathered here to provide death in overabundance." Now we no longer need the extras.

In The Atomic Cafe, *a found-footage film on the growth of nuclear peril, there's a striking scene in which you see a group of American soldiers marching, bayonets forward, toward an atomic mushroom slowly rising several miles ahead. It was the last parade, the last puppet show in the Guignol Theater of war.*

We are facing a cult. That's why I spoke of idolatry. Pure War is the absolute idol. If technological progress has brought ideologies in place of the aims of war, as Raymond Aron said, the scientific progress of nuclear energy is bringing idolatry in place of ideologies. Because nuclear war is an idolatry. Pure War is a situation which is entirely comparable to that of the idol in ancient societies. We've come back to the supreme idol.

—Paris-New York, January–June, 1982

INFOWAR

The End of Bipolarity □ General History and Eventual History □
Sciences of the Extreme □ Fascist Delirium □ Terrorism Large
and Small □ The World Trade Center □ The Art of Technology
or the End of Art □ A Formless War □ The Logistics of Communication □ The Accident □ LA was a Riot □ Radioactivity and
Interactivity □ Open Sky □ Collaboration or Resistance □ The
Militarization of Science □ World Time

Paul Virilio: Things have happened since we last saw each other.
The world has changed so much it has become boring. That's new,
at any rate (*laughs*). I suppose America is the same. It's not getting
any better?

Sylvère Lotringer: *No, not really. The dismantling of the Welfare
State is continuing. The safety net is being let go. People are tightening
their belts, or at least those who own one. But hands off the military
budget. It's endo-colonization at its best. Although* Pure War *was
published in 1983, some fifteen years ago, most of the topics we dealt
with then are still current. The only thing that seems to have obviously
changed is the end of the cold war, the collapse of the Soviet Empire and*

of the logic of bipolarity. And then the proliferation of local conflicts: in ex-Yugoslavia and in Rwanda, etc. You have just published a collection of topical essays, A Landscape of Events, *which turns out to deal exactly with that period between 1984 and 1996 that we're covering now.*[16] *How did it feel to go over that chronicle of the last twelve years? Any big surprise?*

A Landscape of Events is a countdown. I turn the clock back on the events. I start with an article called "Revolution: Day 1," where I come to some conclusions about what has just happened in 1996, then we trace things backwards, '96, '95, back to 1984. I ordered them so that you get a sense of the modification of history. The point of the book, and where the title comes from, is that it's a travelogue in time, composed backwards, not chronologically, so that you get an impression of shifting reality, with the end of deterrence, relations with the city, etc. I'm pleased with the book, but it's more of an impressionistic work. It collapses 12 years in which absolutely everything happened. Between 1984 and 1996 we saw it all: not only the Berlin wall, the implosion of the Soviet Union and the Gulf war, but also small, microscopic events, like Daboville's circumnavigation in a rowboat and the bombing of the World Trade Center, etc. So it's also a book that tries to show that eventual history broke down in favor of general history. General history is all about long stretches of time, and so Braudel, Bloch, and the *École des Annales* are right, primacy has passed from general history to eventual history. Local time has won over.

Everyone is lamenting the disappearance of history, but in your preface you declare that now we're saturated with the past.

Exactly. This book tries to show that we no longer come to terms with the future, because we're really anchored in the present, the present of real time, an instant present. We're not extending ourselves to the future anymore, our only points of reference are located in the past. That's where we get the fear of the past, the fear that the past will return.

The past is full of events that are no longer very eventful.

Quite.

Do you think that this "landscape of events," or the twelve years that have passed since the publication of Pure War *have altered the picture we drew together back then, or do you see that as a simple twist to "Pure War"?*

No, in any case Pure War is linked to science. In any final analysis Pure War wasn't tied down to the confrontation between East and West, but to the development of science as *technoscience*. What has been forgotten is that during the period of deterrence, science became technoscience, that is, experimental science became one with technology. It became a sort of art for art's sake of science. Performance replaced philosophical reflection. Technology performing for its own sake finally legitimated science. The division that existed between science and philosophy, in the eighteenth century say, was exploded with the advent of deterrence. With Nobel Prizes, the military industrial complex and so forth, science has become a kind of science of the extreme.

It brings to mind—to furnish an image for this—extreme sports which are sports where one dices with death: sports for performance's sake, but often a performance that is solitary, in the sense that there is no comparing it to anything save the risk of a warranted death. Technoscience is of that kind, it seems to me: it dices with the death of science by its extremist tendencies. You can see that in the field of genetics and the acceptance of genetically engineered products in Europe, for example. There is, therefore, a kind of scientific delirium. Science's cutting loose, science has become a race to the death, as someone said.

You might say that bipolarisation introduced a form of regulation, or of regularization. It fueled a confrontation but drew back from going too far. Now that all forms of regulation of this type have disappeared...

Absolutely. And so, in a certain sense, science is free to indulge its highest aspirations. That is what was said about the Fascists. Fascists are those who go to the end of their aspirations. Extreme sports are Fascist sports. And a science of the extremes is a Fascist science. Across the spectrum of knowledge, including the computer revolution, we are engaged in this kind of delirium, the delirium of a science of pure performance. Whence my reference to the *speed of liberation*, namely, dare me and I'm off. Off where?

And yet all the conflicts that we have witnessed seem to have entered phases of negotiation and reconciliation, as happened with the confrontation between the two power blocs. Consider the Arab-Israeli conflict, the Balkans, South Africa, Guatemala, and Haiti. There were no escalations to any extremes there, and it's not true of the nuclear race either. It didn't turn out to be the worst-case nuclear scenario...

Unless the worst-case scenario is nuclear terrorism. As far as deterrence goes, regulation used to impede proliferation: you could retaliate against your adversary by raising the stakes in a kind of game. But as soon as nuclear arms start proliferating there can be no more deterrence. We're beyond deterrence. In a certain sense, then, nuclear arms are no longer subject to regulation. They can go off anywhere.

Deterrence was still a kind of humanist restraining order. You recognized your adversary for what it was, and could do. You could predict its reactions. You could always count on it to avoid the worst-case.

Yes, it was a game, a military game, a *Kriegspiel.* Whereas now the Kriegspiel doesn't exist anymore. It now goes from small-scale terrorism, like Black September which blows up aircraft, and to larger-scale terrorism, like the World Trade Center and Oklahoma City bombings, and the Aum Shinrykio gassing in Japan, for example—gas in the subway is a form of civilian terrorism. And so too is the hostage-taking of 700 people at the Japanese embassy in Lima, except that this is taking it to another stage. I'm tempted to say that what we can expect now is the hijacking of an entire town, and that is the classic scenario of nuclear terrorism, and of nuclear proliferation.

America is well-aware of this and this is what panics her. With the end of the cold war both the US and Russia now have large stocks of plutonium on hand and recently there was a big debate within the Administration about ways of disposing of it. The Department of Energy recommended that plutonium from dismantled atomic bombs be used as fuel in civilian nuclear power plants before being discarded as nuclear waste, but other agencies strongly objected because it would make it easier for terrorists or "rogue states" to steal or use it for nuclear weapons. The National Academy of Sciences finally recommended to

the National Security Agency that they "vitrify" plutonium with oxides,
then contaminate it with highly radioactive waste, but the risks of
plutonium disposal and weapons proliferation remain formidable.

Absolutely, but they can't do anything about it. The former Soviet
Union is in such a state that fissile material is being moved around
God knows where.

Some has already been stolen. At least six thefts of nuclear material
have been intercepted abroad. We don't even know if that's the lot....

And it's worth reminding ourselves that nuclear weapons do not
need to be exploded to be terrorizing, all it takes is that they contaminate one area and force an evacuation. Chernobyl wasn't an
explosion in the strictest sense of the word, and what a drama that
was. A little Chernobyl somewhere or contamination with nuclear
waste, or any leak—not even a significant one—would suffice,
where a whole city or a region would have to be evacuated. For my
money, we have entered an age of large-scale terrorism. Just as we
speak of petty delinquency and major delinquency, I think the
same could be said of petty and major terrorism. Small-scale terrorism happens in Northern Ireland, where bombs blow up a car
and can kill one hundred people. The large-scale version is a totally different matter. The World Trade Center was an initial
indication of this, a kind of Hiroshima. Don't forget: the WTC
bomb is just like Hiroshima, and this takes us to the next stage.
Oklahoma followed suit. Terrorist deaths used to be counted in
their hundreds, now suddenly it could jump to 20,000 dead. I was
asked to investigate the WTC blast. If the van had managed to park
at the base of the tower, instead of the access ramp, the whole Trade

Center would have gone up. In what way, we can't imagine. But there would have been 10,000, 20,000 dead; in other words, the equivalent of a strategic cruise missile strike. The Iraqi War didn't go that far. Ten to twenty thousand deaths is the equivalent of a full-scale military operation. A mere five men and a van, but a well-positioned van would have done it.

Let's go back to the idea of "Pure War" because it seems as though it's even more the order of the day than it was fifteen years ago.

It is certainly the order of the day, but it has gone into science. The military-industrial and scientific complexes continue to function on their own momentum. It's a crazy engine that won't stop.

And is there an art of that engine?

The Vision Machine[17] dealt with that question: What are machines for seeing? What is a visionless gaze? Next is *The Art of the Motor*,[18] an art that would simply be an art of technology, and this would mean the end of art. Not the end of art in Baudrillard's sense, but the end in that technology has become the last art, and that includes perception. With a machine that sees for itself. From now on, art goes via the engine. It begins with the filmmaker's clapper board. You can't understand what has happened to cinema, the seventh art, without the art of the engine. The aesthetics of disappearance[19] is changing gears. It's going via motorization. And what's going on is a lot more than this motorization that was analyzed in terms of film criticism or video art. This art of the engine is unprecedented, it's the art of virtual reality. It's therefore an art of stereophony, of sonic depths. The robotization of art is not simply about small objects that beep, like Tinguely's machines, it's actually the assumption of art in technoscience. But it's also a terminal figure. In the same way as we said at the start that technoscience is Pure War, a frightful thing, technoscience can also tend towards becoming art. It's the flip side. And through infowar, this is the game that is afoot. The information theater plays upon the question of *techné*, the robotics of art, namely, art at one with technology.

So technology is asymptotic to everything.

I have always said that. When someone says to me, "I don't understand your position," my response is, "I'll explain it to you: I am a critic of the art of technology." Fair enough? That's all. If they still don't understand, then I say: "Just look at what an art critic is to traditional art, and then substitute technology for traditional art, and you have my position." It's that simple.

Traditional art used to inscribe itself in space; now real space has been replaced by real time.

Real time reigns supreme. That's why music is the art of reference, that is, an art of time and acceleration. It's an art of time and speed. It's even the first to have given form to speed. It's not by chance that young people only have one art, and that's music. It carries the rest of them with it. It's extraordinary that the only thing that stands in the way of television is music.

Music is more and more linked to technology. The hottest music to date is techno, industrial....

Techno, synthesizing, etc.

Lets go back to Pure War. In the States they declared at first that they would reduce the military budget…

And they aren't reducing it.

No, of course they aren't. They savagely cut social programs, but no-one spoke up when the defense budget was being discussed… It's as if it were a non-issue.

Of course, that's to be expected.

Yet elsewhere around the globe significant reductions in military budgets have been made. And that isn't counting the Soviet Union which hadn't the option.

There is also uncertainty about the enemy. Every war is original because it defines its enemy. He is never always exactly the same. A civil war doesn't have the same type of enemy as a national, international, or global war. Today the enemy is unclear. But the enemy is, of course, the terrorist. It's not talked about, but every one knows that he's the threat.

And the countries that provide support, like Libya, Iran, Syria…

Yes. There are those states who support terrorism, but that isn't enough to determine the form of a conflict. What is specific about terrorism is that it is a formless war. Take the war in ex-Yugoslavia, it was game over the day the Croats succeeded in engaging and defeating the Serbs in open battle. At that point the allies intervened and closed everything down. As long as they were slugging it out in nasty little firefights, nothing could be done. In order that a war be a war, it has to have a form, otherwise it turns into a civil war, a war against oneself. Now at this stage, the world situation is characterized by domestic war, and linked to a domestic situation. There is no overt enemy. The Americans, or the Pentagon, are the self-declared great power, but a great power with no enemy—no *designated* enemy (I purposely use designate). You cannot really claim to be a great power.

Which means that no power can be truly great from this point on, as had been the case 'til now. That too, is a change of level.

Yet, absolutely. And the United States are very threatened by their own supremacy. They don't know where they are.

But the WTC case wasn't even a nuclear threat, or an acceleration of speed.

No. Terrorism uses the speed of mass communication. Let's remind ourselves that terrorism needs the media. If you manage to blow up the WTC without anyone knowing about it, that's pointless. The same goes for 10,000 people dead and no one batting an eyelid. The problem is that when two people are killed in Somalia and they happen to be Americans, it's a national drama. You see that terrorism anticipated the information war described by the Pentagon, which is now preparing a revolution in military matters based on infowar and the infosphere. The first to have waged such an information war were the terrorists. They scheduled their bomb-blast on time to catch the evening news. The explosion only exists because it is simultaneously coupled to a multimedia explosion. What is more, the WTC is a teleport, a communications center. An economic and communications center.

On the other hand, in Iraq, the poison gas didn't explode, it mostly went unnoticed. And later, when people began to suffer from it, there has been hardly any reaction from the media, nor from the public...

Those affected were the Kurdish villages.

So it's not the power of the explosion itself but the media explosion that matters.

Yes. You might say that during the period of deterrence the media developed because actual nuclear blasts had been frozen and delivery systems, further enhanced by means of the satellite, guidance systems and smart technology's pinpointing targets, so the capacity to gather information in real time had no limits. Today therefore, the end of deterrence corresponds to the beginning of the information war, a conflict where the superiority of information is more important than the capability to inflict damage. This is an entirely new situation. We're entering a third age of military weaponry.

What were the others?

The first weapons system was determined by *obstruction*, that is to say, ramparts, shields, the size of the elephant. It's like warding off the small-fry aggressor with a dismissive swat. You don't even need to slap him in the face. Arms of obstruction were the first instruments of war from the outset. Next came weapons of *destruction*, particularly artillery which changed everything, and up to thermonuclear devices. And destructive power blocked nuclear war by means of deterrence. The third series of weapons systems, though, has not been neutralized, and that's the weaponry of *communication*.

And that weaponry you call a logistics of communication.

That's what interests me. Weapons of communication had been in at the start with spies, messengers, and signals like the Indian smoke signal, and so forth. But there has been no really significant development since the Chappe telegraph in Napoleon's time. It took the period of deterrence for everything to take off. Besides, that corresponds to the development of information technology, the invention of the computer, satellites' capacity to transmit information instantly, and to the advent of the C3i—there are four of them now—namely, Control, Command, Intelligence, C3i, the war room, which is the body that anticipates war because it anticipates the profile of the enemy. I remind you of Goebbels' phrase: "He who knows everything is not afraid of anything." It's an incredible statement, because Goebbels is a man of information. Maybe not of information in the computer age, but of information all the same. And that's exactly what the Americans are trying to do. In my opinion, they are misguided. For that sentence offers only a relative truth…

One can never anticipate everything. There can always be a surprise in store, or an "act of God," if you will.

Yes. And you know about my pet project that will be my next book: *The Accident*. My book on the accident will be the *fin-de-siécle* book. Thank God, and I mean it, there is the reverse of the miracle, the accident, which can happen any time and isn't predictable by definition.

You have always written your books in series.

I don't do it deliberately, it just naturally works out that way. It's not a desire to write books, in fact it's events that set them off and running. The book on the accident has been on-the-go for at least ten years.

Meanwhile there have been quite a few accidents. The latest were the Los Angeles riots. They took everyone by surprise.

Yes. Were you there?

I was travelling through the East Coast and I was glued to the radio and television. As soon as the riot began there was an incredible media blitz: everything had to be explained away: Watts, poverty, gangs, with community leaders, priests, and sociologists called to the mic.... Everything except the surprise of the event. I arrived in Los Angeles towards the end of the riots, and I was very struck by the light-heartedness and energy that prevailed. People were breathing more freely, rediscovering politics, helping in other neighborhoods, or raiding supermarkets... Not a word of that in the media. Blight and despair is more reassuring, joy is a threat. I wanted to interview people, put together a fast book. I had a great title: "LA was a Riot." But the police had already begun to subpoena every testimony... And yet, as in May '68, you're left to wonder if this accident was turned to the future or already a thing of the past. Revolution is no longer the order of the day...

When one attempts to develop weapons of communication the possibility of a new type of accident arises. In the fifties, when Einstein met the Abbé Pierre[20]—yes, they met, the Abbé Pierre told me himself—what did Einstein say to him? He told him that there are three kinds of bomb. The first is the *atomic* bomb, and we know what that is: deterrence begins right there; the second is the information explosion; he didn't say computer, since the word didn't yet exist, but I can call it an explosion in *computer technology*. And the third will be the *demographic* explosion, which is to say the exponential population boom. Now, if we take Einstein's term rather than the Pentagon's, waging an information war means the setting off of the technology bomb. In other words, information doesn't merely transmit or conmunicate the news, facts, but rather deals with interactivity and organization.

I remind you that the atom bomb is about radioactivity, or more precisely, organizing it so that there's an explosion, fusion, fission, or pollution. Now, the technology bomb isn't just used for information technology, it also involves *interactivity* to a degree one can't even imagine; feedbacks whose consequences one can't even fathom since we've never seen that before. Like the atom bomb, in fact. It is another kind of accident than nuclear accidents such as the melt-downs at Three Mile Island and Chernobyl. It's an information accident.

Orson Welles' War of the Worlds...

Yes, exactly. No longer an accident involving an explosion, or radioactivity, but interactivity among people. And that's unknown territory.

It's some kind of information panic...

Yes, tangentially. My next book will deal with anticipation. It will be the first of its kind, even. For once, I'm going to try to forecast this integral accident. The word "integral" is very important.

Have there already been events that foreshadow this integral accident?

Only one: the stock market crash. It isn't enough, but it is a fore-taste in the sense that it simultaneously happened everywhere. It is no longer localized as a specific accident, it is not located where the "Titanic" sank, or Chernobyl leaked, but it is everywhere. In this regard, it's much like the bomb that goes off. Boom. But what is it that booms? We don't even know. It's a phenomenon…

A phenomenon of instant saturation, or a kind of vitrification of the world?

We have to work hard to know what it is because is has never happened before. The atomic bomb went beyond the competence of the military staffs and that's why they came up with deterrence. You could reduce or increase the bomb in size, but it went beyond them—deterrence is the fruit of nuclear power. Once the information bomb is recognized as such, as a power that overwhelms military staffs, it may well be that a number of states, America, but certainly Japan and Europe as well, will impose a form of information deterrence, a societal deterrence. No longer nuclear deterrence, preventing the use of such weapons, but deterring the masses faced with flashpoint situations. I don't think it will take long before the information bomb is recognized as such. The delirium surrounding the Internet is rather instructive in this respect.

Can we call that a paroxysmal form of propaganda?

Oh, but it's more than that. You can't even use the term. For there to be deterrence, there has to be an initial fallout from the explosion, or from this accident.

We are in the unknown.

Certainly we're in the unknown. First of all, nuclear proliferation means that from now on, nuclear weapons are readily available to everyone. I'm not joking either. In one generation—I never speak in terms of the immediate present—everyone will have nuclear weapons. Big, small, whatever. In a sense, then, it's already here. No, the question I ask concerns the nature of a weapon of communication that perfects itself to the point of calling for deterrence. Deterrence of information and interactivity. By way of an example: when the Wall Street crash happened in 1987 it was generally assumed that it was *program trading*, the automatic quotation of stock values, that had accelerated and propagated the crash. The Swiss stepped back first from the Big Bang—that's what it is called, this global stock quoting—declaring that they weren't playing that sort of game, that short-circuits had to be found. Whenever automatic quoting becomes erratic, as happened then, you have to go back to manual, like the pilot who manually takes over from the automatic pilot when things go wrong in an aircraft. So they now have kinds of circuit-breakers which take care of that. As soon as the automatic system messes up, they switch to a back-up control system. I think we have a situation there that tomorrow will be applied by military planners. But one cannot tell yet, because one doesn't know what interactivity will mean on a global scale. We are only at the start. The Internet is only a side road compared to the highway that the real Web will become, a Web that will be controlled by the military. And don't tell me that the Internet will bring about world democracy. I split my sides at that. There's nothing more ridiculous. The Internet is just a product sample for the electronic highways. The real Web that's in the offing will become a war-machine in the sense that Deleuze understands it of course. So I don't think we know what interactivity is. As long as we don't, we cannot protect ourselves against its accident. There is a lot of work to be done on the notion of feedback, interactivity among people, populations, continents, and so forth. As happened with globalization, we're caught in something we can't control.

That's what your latest book deals with, La Vitesse de libération *[Liberation Speed].*

In *Liberation Speed*, twenty years or so after *Speed and Politics*,[21] I reintroduced the word "speed." I remind you that *liberation speed* is a technical notion, 28,000 km/h: it's the speed you need to reach orbit. 40,000 km/h is *escape velocity*. You don't just need to go into orbit, but also to escape orbit in order to go to the moon. I took liberation speed because it seems as though the two important velocities are the speed limit, of course, lightspeed, which allows for telecommunications, feedback, the information bomb, etc., and also liberation speed, which permits man to free himself from his world and escape Earth. It's an incredible speed, the one that frees us from our own world. I don't think that we've studied it enough.

And is it a real liberation?

I understand liberation in its technical sense, but it's a bit of a joke for me. It's nothing like a liberation. The English title will be *Open Sky*, because someone had already taken the title "Escape Velocity." The preface is about Open Sky, the idea that liberation speed is a means of puncturing the sky. Free fall upward. Upward and downward: nowadays we do both. So the English title works.

It's the only door that remains open.

Yes, but one that leads to the sidereal void, to the uninhabitable, in other words. Don't forget that I've always dealt with habitats. I'm no ecologist in the Green Party sense, but I'm still all for the habitat: there's no man without it.

And is the sky a habitat?

It's still a habitat. But when it's been pierced, no. It leaks away. So *Open Sky* is a book that deals with this emancipation, and the one we're in at the moment, namely, globalization.

You wrote an article in the newspaper Libération *called "L'accident originel" [The Original Accident]. Was it about this reverse miracle, what accident could be in a globalization situation?*

In this article I said that the accident is to the human sciences what sin is to human nature. In other words, technology is defective, like the human sciences. They have a defect, like we do. But this defect is our greatness too. We are human because we are defective.

So technology can never be pure.

No. That's the attempt by the *Deus ex machina*. The great idol. The great combat is between transcendent God and God-machine. We should be able to talk about this, but we can't. It's not politically correct. I can talk about it with Christians, but not with anyone else. And I'm fed up with that. We should be able to talk about sex, angels, God, everything. The world has arrived at an extremity where things need to be sorted out. Have they survived the fire, or what? When do we cut the umbilical cord? We're backed into a corner too, you see. All of us. Not simply a deathly impasse, but stuck in the corner as a result of globalization and everything we've been describing. It's the end of an era. It's the end of a temporal regime, and hence a regime of thought. Philosophy was inscribed in historical time, whereas today, in the new historical time, this real time has no thought. It can have non-thought, in other words, a negation. Nihilism could be its Assumption in times to come, far beyond what Fascism and Nazism were, and that's the great tempta-tion. In that case, you can't be a collaborator. That's why I'm saying that you can collaborate or resist faced with this situation. The thing about collaborators is that you don't know you are one, whereas as member of the resistance, you do. To be in the resistance, you choose to be in it. If I take the Second World War as an example, the worst cases of collaboration weren't among the real collaborators, the official Militia, but among the populace at large, who were collaborators without knowing it, by a sort of laxity, an apathy.

But is this Great Combat the only option? Maybe there will be an accident of this new type and other modes of regulation will be intro-duced at once, as happened during the stock market crash. Politics don't always bring about the very worst, even the worst case is far more instructive on what can happen.

Perhaps. But don't forget that the Pentagon considers information a weapon. We are then in a situation involving Secret Defense. Today, the real place worth scrutinizing is the National Security Agency, not the CIA or FBI—and let's hear no more about the CIA and FBI, they're stale. But no-one talks very much about the NSA and that's where the game is played out, the veritable revolution in military doctrine, wargaming with information, the ongoing game in the corridors of military power. You know that I am acquainted with military people, on my side of the Atlantic, and I assure you that they're very interested by all this. I received an invitation the other day to brief them on all this, and I told them you must be joking. You can buy my books, I'm not going to advertise them for you. Look out for yourselves, it's your job. You've got medals on your chest. I've got none, or next to none. Only sergeant's stripes (*laughs*). And I'm not proud of them either (*laughs*).

In Nevada there is a place called Area 51. I drove there with my wife, Chris Kraus. It's an unmarked road in the desert and finally you get to an area that's immense, the size of three small East Coast states, and there is just a sign that says: "Beyond this point anything can happen." I stopped, I spotted video cameras in the cactus plants, and a white jeep driving up with men in white. They said nothing, simply stopped about three hundred meters away and waited for me to make the first move and go beyond the sign. People disappear this way, or they blow their tires out. It's a private militia that patrols Area 51, and they aren't controlled by anyone. Tests on the Stealth bombers and other new prototypes are carried out there, and nuclear experiments, disposing of nuclear waste, and so forth.

The Soviets used to do that as well.

And theoretically, this base doesn't exist. The Pentagon categorically denied its existence.

We've entered the era of the militarization of science. In a sense, these are sciences of the extreme. Science itself has become Pure War, and it no longer needs enemies. It has invented its own goal. I'm going to spend two or three years trying to figure out this situation which also involves absolute speed. I'm back to my dromological problems. Why involve speed? Because the limits of speed have been reached. Except for computing speed, where there is still progress to be made, with photonic and quantic computers replacing electronic computers, computer technology has reached its limits, some 300,000 km/sec. There is no going beyond that. We are in the realm of the infraluminic, as it is called, and the question then becomes: what is a society that has reached the limits of speed and therefore views speed as an unsurpassable dimension of the State's history and of human history? So, in a sense, the limit has been reached, and Fukuyama is entirely wrong: it's not the end of history, but the end of a regime of historical temporality. All of history was inscribed in local time, in local space and time. Time in China is not the same as time in Europe, just as time in Paris is not time in Aix-en-Provence, and so on. Now the history that is beginning is synchronized to world time, in other words, it's happening "live." What prevails is not the local time of time zones, or the passage from night into day, but the time as Hamlet, quoted by Deleuze, defined it: "Time out of joint." That's world time right there. Reaching the speed of light and using it to take a leak, now that's a major event.

—Translated by Brian O' Keeffe

Postscript, 2007

WAR ON THE CITIES

1

The New Bunkers

Metropolitics □ War on Civilians □ Dead-End Corridors □ Claustropolis □ Vertical Bunkers □ Suicidal Soldiers □ Real Time Tyranny □ A Communism of Affects □ May 1968 □ Power to the Imagination □ The WTC □ Power to the Image □ Architects' Intelligence □ Construction and Destruction □ Carpet Bombardment □ Time Out of Joint □ Cardboard Reality □ The University of Disaster

Sylvère Lotringer: *In 1983, you were convinced that war would be either nuclear war, or nothing. Twenty-five years later, we are still confronted with the same alternative, but after globalization, war has gone global too. The nuclear threat is only one aspect of the Total War now imposed on urban populations. With the rise of asymmetrical warfare, Total War has become local on an international scale. The city is the new battlefield. Attacking one automatically threatens them all. We've seen this happen with New York, London, and Madrid…*

Paul Virilio: This is what happens when one moves from a geopolitical to a metro-political era. You can see signs of this everywhere. This morning, for example,[22] I noticed in the paper that Bernard

Kouchner[23] came up with the idea of using humanitarian corridors to evacuate the population in Darfur. We've gone from military war to intra-military war, to traditional civil war—and finally to war *on civilians*. Civilians are no longer even hostages, they have become the enemy to destroy. It's become obvious with the collapse of the World Trade Center, but in Lebanon as well cities are being bombed whenever one can claim the presence of Hezbollah. So what is it that Kouchner is proposing now? Humanitarian corridors.

What else is happening today? The Lebanese army. They've been fighting in a Palestine refugee camp for a whole month and they made what they call a "breakthrough." Three people killed… And I couldn't help thinking: "Nonsense!" In former times, it took a major tank offensive in the great plains of Russia for people to talk about a breakthrough. An army that doesn't manage to subdue a suburb in one month is no longer an army. Now Gaza. They say that Palestinians are trying to get the hell out of the enclave; obviously, they're not crazy about living under the Islamists' rule. Now you'll understand why I'm interested in all that; right now they're rushing into this concrete corridor that is still open between Israel and Gaza. And I made a note to myself: this is the new bunker. *The bunker as passage.* You have the humanitarian corridor and the concrete corridor. See how everything's changed. Bunkers used to be places of shelter, or places from where they could fire on allied ships along the Atlantic coast; now they've become corridors of concrete. The new bunker is a passage from one place to another. It makes you think of "gated communities" in the United States, which you know about as well as I, not mentioning Latin America, the Alphavilles in São Paolo, etc. There are even some starting up in France.

We're now dealing with dead-end corridors.

Exactly. What I called claustropolis has replaced cosmopolis, where I'm from, since I'm the son of an illegal Italian immigrant *in France*. On the other hand, in Shanghai, in China, they're the avant-garde of modernity, in terms of claustropolis: *towerism*. They've got 4,000 towers over there. Towers aren't just a matter of prestige. They're super-gated; except for Spiderman, no one is climbing up their facades.

Towers are vertical bunkers.

High-altitude impasses. No one goes through, except in altitude. The Chinese today are enforcing urbanization. They're moving people allegedly dangerous for the ecology, and forcing them to live in cities. We're really witnessing a mutation of the State and the Nation-State, a mutation of the city.

When terrorists attack cities, they're merely speeding up a mutation that is already underway.

First of all, they've realized that the city has replaced the nation, that we've gone back to the City-State. Let's recall that the history of the state begins with the Greek City-State, a gathering of villages; this was the fortified city, the fortress of the Middle Ages; then it became the capital of the Nation-State, the city of cities.

Terrorists assault the city from inside, *replacing massive bombings of the anti-city strategy with selective human-bombs.*

They also trigger bombs by mobile phone. Synchronization on the one hand, on the other delays between every major event, every attack; all this shows that there's some real intelligence behind it all. One would think they'd launch their attacks in a series, one following closely on another; but no, they have a sense of timing. They wait for the right moment. In my opinion, delaying is part of their strategy.

If they detonated a bomb every two or three months, it would be too much—it would trigger a backlash.

Well, then, it's surprising we continue to be so anxious while waiting. The attacks must always be unexpected. If the intervals were too regular, there could be a response, a riposte; you're quite right, there would be a backlash, a revolt. In this sense we're dealing here with theatre, a ritual drama. Theatre is very prominent in such situations. First of all, you cast the actors. Verdun or Stalingrad were classical wars; there were no actors, only masses facing each other. (Not to mention generals, of course: Rommel in Tobruk, Paulus in Stalingrad, etc.) Terrorism, on the other hand, has actors, but they're hardly personalized—ordinary people, just suicidal types. This also is a major distinction: The Suicidal Soldier is something new. Before, the soldier was putting his life on the line, he did not lay it down.

Suicide has already been used as a war weapon. One just played death against death.

Yes, but it mostly came from Japan. Strangely enough, this hasn't been discussed much. We've heard plenty about Hiroshima, Nagasaki, but not of the national suicide project of Japan. If it were not for Hirohito, who was a fairly intelligent individual, the militarists would have carried out a national suicide: an entire country committing mass suicide.

Hitler didn't shy away from that either.

In Japan's case, it was even more drastic, I would say, since there was a religious dimension attached. Hitler wanted to suicide the country rather than order it to commit suicide; the national suicide of Japan was to be a collective pact, not at all the same thing. This was alien to our culture, even to Nazi culture; and the Japanese contaminated the Arab world through a woman from the Japanese Red Army, it seems —"The Red Princess"—who became the lover of a Palestinian terrorist. This is an interesting case of cultural influence.

Death wasn't something private and suicides relied on a precise ritual. It was theatre, but of another kind, closer to Antonin Artaud's theatre of cruelty. One identified with the wound.

For sure, Brecht and Artaud. I wrote a book called *Ground Zero*, the French name of which, *Ce qui arrive* (What Happens) gave its name to my exhibition on accidents at the Fondation Cartier in Paris, in 2002–2003. For accidents are literally "what happens." I quoted Brecht on the back cover of the book: "They've been hiding something from us, but the curtain is going up." I wrote this in 2001. A community of passions is fundamentally theatrical. A theatre is a place of shared emotions, as is the case with a Greek tragedy or a great film. On that score, the movie house is a pre-figuration of the end of political assembly, where speech and the word ruled.

The birth of tragedy was the beginning of democracy.

The Birth of Tragedy was a book Nietzsche didn't care for; but for me it is his only book. Nietzsche was not a great philosopher, but a great poet; and I find tragedy in the anonymous murmuring chorus passing judgment on what's happening onstage between the heroes, Antigone, etc., commenting the action for the audience; all that I find truly wonderful. The ancient Chorus is the beginning of democracy.

All of that was replaced by special effects on the big or little screen.

That's where battles are fought today. The battlefield of the terrorists, but of "heroes" as well, cultural or otherwise. The tyranny of real time has replaced the tyranny of real space. These are our great empires of today. When you see the impact of the attack of 2001, eleven guys with the planes they hijacked, not even bombers, but civilian aircraft; and then of the tsunami, which had nothing to do with it, a catastrophe, there's a world synchronization of international public emotion. This is an absolutely wondrous event, something really colossal that an emotion can be shared at the same instant by billions of individuals. There has never been anything like it. Total War was just a kiddies' game compared with this! This is also a powerful phenomenon that terrorists use to the maximum; and in order to carry this out, they need to affect a maximum number of people at the same moment; the city is the ideal and fatal place for it. If you provoked an immense catastrophe in the middle of the Sahara, even if you turned half the desert into glass, no one would pay the slightest attention.

The great events of our time, May '68, September 11, also were theatre. But the script was quite different.

May '68 was a very complex thing. Even if barricades went up, there was no revolution to speak of, not even a riot, and yet there were events all the same. "The *events* of 1968": I find those words very appropriate. Pierre Grimaud, the Paris police commissioner, was a cultivated man, thank God, and he made sure there wouldn't be too much damage. In his memoirs he wrote: "May 1968 was the last literary revolution in Europe." I couldn't agree more. Of course, there were Trotskyites, Maoists, Alain Krivine,[24] Che Guevara, etc., but there was especially Surrealism, Situationism. It belonged to a very literary and theatrical vision of Europe, of a crepuscular Europe, as my friend Jean Duvignaud[25] used to say. He happened to be at the Odéon Theatre with me when it all started. May 1968 was not the beginning of something, but an end-point.

It was not a theatre of cruelty, but another scene.

No, not at all, it was a theatre of the mind...

...a theatre of imagination; you could still believe it was possible to innovate. Society could be an artwork, a performance. The crowd in the street was the chorus. It was the last creative reaction against consumerism.

"Power to the imagination," is what I wanted to say.

Are you the one who wrote that famous motto? It was attributed to the Situationists.

No, it was me who made the poster. I tacked it on the doors of the Chapel at the Sorbonne; then it was taken over elsewhere, when we stormed the Odéon. Power to the imagination. That was the end of a world.

The end of direct democracy. Now there's nothing left to attack and nothing to defend. Baudrillard was right about the images from Abu Ghraib: "Those who live by the spectacle will die by the spectacle."

In any case the best defense is to attack; and to attack you must have some ideas; right now there aren't any ideas. Imagination today is in the image, and the image is in power. There's no imagination for anything but the image.

The World Trade Center attack also was meant for the image.

Absolutely! *Only* for the image; and following an architect's ritual. Mohammed Atta was an architect who got his diploma in Alexandria, but as this diploma cost nothing and was of no use whatsoever, he got a second degree at Hamburg, a city that was destroyed in a hurricane of fire, like Dresden. I tried to obtain a copy of his diploma, since it's amazing—he used his diploma to demolish the towers. There wasn't just an organization behind it, it was planned with an architect's intelligence and a strategic understanding of the situation. In France, when you build a tower there has to be a concrete core to protect the elevators and serve as a trunk for the floors. This is a technical matter. The World Trade Center towers had no central core. It's no surprise that the first attack already targeted the foundations; they were after the same thing. I teach architecture, so I understood this right away.

Are you sure they realized it?

I have no doubt about it. Atta meant to collapse the World Trade Center, I'm positive. If he had managed to blow up the foundations, it would have had the same effect, except for an additional possibility, which I mentioned in *New York Delirium*, in reference to Rem Koolhas. Imagine the Twin Towers collapsing on their own weight, it would have been four or five thousand, maybe ten thousand dead. These were the numbers I came up with in 1996, six or seven years before September 11. So there was a technical intelligence behind all this, Mohammed Atta's and probably others. Atta should be researched as the mastermind of the project; but he hasn't been.

An architect attacking architecture, builder and destroyer all in one, is this something exceptional?

Albert Speer was an architect. Architects are always close to the prince. Architecture is at the service of power. There is no such thing as a monarch without architect, whether to erect his tomb, pyramids, or palaces; the architect's power is a major political power.

There's a certain relation to death in that.

Architects work against destruction. We call that the statics and resistance of materials. One of the first things that architects learn at school is statics and resistance. They learn at the same time about destruction and construction. It's learning in reverse. There is always a special relation between constructor and destructor. You can't make a good shield if you do not know about the lance. This is how you go about constructing a battlefield. It must be created before it is destroyed. And today the battlefield is cities. It is no coincidence that in France, this year, we're celebrating the 300th anniversary of Vauban, great engineer, architect to the king, and an extraordinary genius.

Vauban tried to minimize the angles of attack by constructing walls in a star pattern. It terms of architecture, you're less interested in construction than in destruction. Therefore in war.

I am a child of war, therefore a man of peace. When Ernst Jünger died, I was asked what I thought of him. And I simply said: "He was a warrior; I a child of war." Not to be confused.

You told me that you lived in Nantes then, and this had a huge impact on you.

I was relocated in Nantes from Paris. I stayed with my maternal grandparents—my mother was a Breton. In 1943 there were two terrifying bombings that destroyed 8,000 buildings and twelve days later squadrons of airplanes returned to level the city.

What nationality were they?

American and English. Except the English had a bit better aim. They were soldiers, taking off from carriers, and it wasn't quite yet the time for "Carpet Bombardment," the tapestry of bombs that levels everything, like in Le Havre, and especially in Dresden. These people were pretty good at bombing. So the city of Nantes was attacked twice horribly, and devastated. I've shown you pictures of the streets.

What was left of them. You couldn't even recognize the buildings. It looked like Berlin, 1945.

It was the war, and we queued up at Lulu, a great biscuit name from Nantes. At the time queuing lasted hours. My mother was going there for the prisoners of war, we sent them packages by mail. She would tell me: "Why don't you wait in line on Calvary Street"—the name was perfect—then she would come back by 11 am and we made some purchases before going back home. One day I walked down Calvary Street in the morning, looking at dime stores; all these toys, great things for a child—and in the afternoon there was absolutely nothing left of it, it had all been leveled. For a child, a city is just like the Alps or the Himalayas, it is there forever. To see in just one afternoon an entire city destroyed is an extraordinary experience. One doesn't believe one's eyes anymore, one becomes a conscientious objector. One can't believe in reality anymore, like our friend Baudrillard. Reality becomes cardboard, a decor that can disappear in the twinkle of an eye.

Have you read Time Out of Joint, *a novel by Philip K. Dick? The hero's task is to solve a crossword puzzle every week in the local newspaper. He doesn't realize that the fate of the world depends on its solution. Then he begins to notice that the village in which he lives had been hastily put together around him so that he could perform his task. It was all cardboard decor, like the half-assed people in President Schreiber's delusions analyzed by Freud. And this world could vanish from one moment to the next.*

I lived through all of that too. In 1943 I was eleven years old, and the world was collapsing all around me, everything was disappearing.

Instantly I became a relativist, I realized that it woud affect my entire life. The bombardment was my university of disaster. The Resistance had scored in a big way by assassinating the Commander General of the Kommandantur in Nantes and the Germans rounded up hostages that they gunned down at Châteaubriant. They took a hostage in the street where I lived. I mentioned that in *The Insecurity of Territory*, my first book besides *Bunker Archeology*. Nantes is very close to the ocean and German sailors would patrol down Rue Saint-Jacques—I showed you the debris in the photographs—Mauser strapped on their shoulder. There was a little girl who lived on the Place de l'Église, a childhood sweetheart. She was nine or ten and she went to the window when she heard the patrol walk by. It was after curfew. A sailor down below shouldered his Mauser and aimed at her. The bullet got her through the eye—he didn't miss. Simply because she was on the terrace. Something you don't forget. I was born there and I'll die there.

2

A Finite World

The War That Never Happened □ Telluric Contractions □ Tyranny and Democracy □ Revolution and Revelation □ Progress and Catastrophe □ Escaping Nihilism □ Scientific Humility □ Natural Proportions □ Pollution of Distances □ Absolute Inertia □ Instantaneity, Ubiquity, Immediacy □ Vision Machines □ Frontal and Lateral □ Perceptive Faith □ The Uncertainty Principle □ The Vertical Littoral

In Pure War *you were the first to assert that peace merely extends war by other means. Logistics cannot be stopped. It requires the continual production of increasingly costly and sophisticated armaments at the expense of civil society. History has confirmed your prognostications. Nuclear deterrence achieved its goal without a single bomb being dropped. The war never happened, and yet it was won. The escalation between the two blocks terminated when one of the adversaries imploded. The Berlin Wall collapsed, clearing the way for the abolition of all obstacles and the global exchange of goods as well as information. Paradoxically, the world that resulted from that wasn't more open, but more closed upon itself. Instead of expanding in space, it contracted in time, and narrowed down. Claustropolis replaced cosmopolis.*

I'd like to think of these as the pains of childbearing, the contractions which prelude delivery; in which case you better have a cab handy to rush the woman to the hospital. Contraction also reminds me of a telluric contraction, an earthquake. I believe that globalization led to a telluric contraction, to moments that herald the birth of a new world, but a finite world. Paul Valéry said: "The time of the finite world is beginning." We're living in the time of the finite world, not of a world about to start. We are about to experience together the time of finitude, the magnitude of the finite world's poverty. This finitude isn't at its beginning—it all started in the eighteenth century, the finitude of the world, with the industrial revolution and those that followed: transportation, energy transmission, and others. Nowadays we're living through the pains and contractions which lead to the delivery of a closed world. This is the closed world that political ecology must confront. The great struggle between tyranny and democracy is going to move from human tyrants—Genghis Khan, or Hitler—to tyranny itself. Tyranny came out of progress, which is what has brought about the tyranny of the end. Progress triggered finitude, transportation, the exhaustion of natural resources, speed, real time, etc. Most people think of speed as progress, they believe that speed simply means going faster from one point to another; but they forget that the world is closing in on us and that we're being asphyxiated by our way of life.

This isn't the type of tyranny one could break away from. It is the tyranny that make us be who we are.

We can't escape it, so we will have to produce a political intelligence of this kind of tyranny. What I'm afraid of is that ideological passéism against progress will become a progressive ideology. The problem of progress is central to understanding the nature of tyranny. That doesn't mean that we should go back to the horse and buggy— you know I don't share this ideal of regressing. Hannah Arendt said that "progress and catastrophe are two sides of the same coin." Progress has become a catastrophe. So we can't avoid confronting the issue of this catastrophe at every single level.

Tyranny is not distinct from democracy either, since it was democracy that brought it about. We might almost say that democracy and tyranny are two sides of the same coin.

At this point I don't know of anyone who would be capable of articulating a clear and positive conception of this situation. Revolution is over; we're entering the era of *revelation*. Revolution is an end, the end of a world and the beginning of another; therefore it's the end of history. Whereas revelation brings out the end of geography, of the end of the earth as an object, but not the end of the world. I would say that we are at the beginning of the "revelation-ary" era. The closure of the world is a revelation. The revelation of finitude is an entirely new situation. This is not the apocalypse. Ideas of the end of the world are of no interest to me. I've said elsewhere: "The end of the world is a concept without a future." What the revelation reveals is that globalization is a finitude. Societies used to rely on local finitudes, frontiers, city ramparts, meta-cities, nations. Nowadays the frontier is the world; the world is finalized. This is an historical event much more important that any revolution. This is not the end of the world, but the realization of its finitude. Hey, it was a joke to say that the discovery of the rotundity of the earth, or of America by Christopher Columbus, was the start of globalization. It's only now that we're really entering into that era, and there simply are no thinkers today who are up to the challenge. The crisis of democracy is a crisis of democratic thought. This is why people like Jacques Rancière[26] are questioning democracy today. Michel Rocard[27] said that the problem with the Socialist Party in France is that Socialists aren't thinking enough. As long as they had Marx, they had it easy…

Thinking is lagging behind because everything now is going too fast. The system itself is doing the thinking for us.

Now it's all going too fast. The question of finitude, in its geo-physical, materialist reality, modifies the content of politics, strategy, ecology. Political ecology must rely on finitude to confront every possible crisis, not only those of the environment, but also of ideas and philosophy. Imagine people like Aristotle, Galileo, or Copernicus in the situation we find ourselves in today. They had no information technology to back up their analyses, no assortment of lenses of any kind, but they had this kind of intelligence. Those were truly amazing times.

Transpolitics mean that we are at the end of the polis, *and of politics as they conceived of it. We're heading to a democracy without democracy, and therefore towards its virtual disappearance.*

In any case, it's an absolute threat to democracy; but here we have to tread very carefully because we're standing on the edge of an abyss. The abyss of nihilism. I said as much when Jean Baudrillard died: "They accused him of being a nihilist because he didn't believe in tele-reality." Me neither, but I am no nihilist for all that. The great challenge, in fact, will be escaping nihilism. Nihilism is no revelation, it's just "*Viva la muerte!*" I believe that there's a hope beyond hope—Saint Paul's phrase—in finitude, in the magnitude of poverty. I believe there is something of the unknown, a *terra incognita* in the logic of poverty. I talked about it in *The Twilight of Spaces* [Le Crépuscule des lieux]. Something's at stake here, something awesome. We didn't realize it because we were too proud, with only conquest in mind. We've even lost any notion of scientific humility! Humility is the very foundation of science. If we don't recognize how little we know, we are unlikely to achieve any knowledge. Acknowledging what we lack is a precondition for science. Science is of humble birth. Whoever says "I know, I know," will never know anything because he already does. So discovering the world's finitude is teaching us philosophically an extraordinary lesson in humility, and we could derive from it a colossal hope. Myself, I'm not at all desperate, rather worried because a kind of madness has replaced "the love of wisdom." This is why I've talked of *philofolly*, rather than philosophy. We're looking at an Babelian epoch, always higher, always faster, until it all collapses. I believe it's time for us to realize that after Babel comes the Deluge. Let's not build up Babel again. Those that say "the earth is flat, let's get on with it," are truly mad. Whether rich or poor, believers or not, makes no difference.

How do you measure this magnitude of poverty?

You've touched on the great question that we are confronting today: the incommensurable. We've forgotten what proportion is. The first thing an architect thinks of is proportion, ratio, scale, degree, as in the formula: *degrees of magnitude*. We've forgotten that nature exists in terms of scale; a 300-feet-high tree is a Sequoia, a tree 15 feet high is a palm tree. An apple is not a pumpkin, and man is not an elephant, etc. Nature exists only according to its own scale, its "simple proportion." It's so extraordinary that we, Westerners, have forgotten that. I would say there's an astounding arrogance and pride in having forgotten the notion of proportion.

The world has grown out of proportion and cannot find its proper size anymore.

Yes, this is paving the way for excess, and then incommensurability, giving rise to the astrophysical ravings of today: "We're going to find exotic planets, furnish them with an artificial atmosphere if they have none, etc." Now we'll be obliged to take proportion into account. Finitude forces commensurability upon us in no uncertain terms. It's all in the NASA photo I've just given you to look at, sphericity, with the caption: "Have you ever dreamt of getting closer to the stars…" There are enormous political, philosophical, economic questions not even raised by the ecology of nature. Implicitly yes, but not politically. I'm amazed whenever I hear ecologists' speeches. OK, agreed about ozone, agreed about pollution, but what about proportion? Along with green ecology, the pollution of substances, and hence of nature—air, water, fauna and flora—it's imperative to take "*gray* ecology," colorless, into account—the pollution of distance and time that speed permits. Whether this is the supersonic speed of planes that changes human relations or the speed of the TGV [French high-speed train] which modifies geography, I've shown that we have to take both pollutions seriously. The ecology of natural proportions is not simply an ecology of nature, but of its scale and proportions. An urbanist is obliged to ask these kinds of questions. There is an art to proportions, geometrical intelligence, "geo" in the sense of geosphere. It's no coincidence that Euclid, Aristotle, the Greeks were not only thinkers but also geometers. You can't separate the West from these two Judeo-Christian and Greco-Latin couples. If you do, sorry, you're throwing out the baby with the bathwater.

Baudrillard talked of the American obese in similar terms. A body has a form, dimensions, symbolic space. Some people have lost all proportion, and no longer inhabit a human form.

You see some who have become empty spheres, are beginning to anticipate sphericity; already experiencing the globalization of the body proper, but not yet that of the world proper; but one foreshadows the other in some way.

This brings us back to what we were saying twenty-five years ago about radical deregulation and the effects it could induce, at once globalization of the body, delocalization of space and disappearance of time. Absolute deregulation tends towards absolute inertia. It is the price paid by capitalist economy.

By all means, but it is an economy that has lost what matters most. The political economy of wealth has simply disregarded the political economy of speed. When you say that time is money, what it means is that speed in time is power. Therefore there are classes of speed like there are classes of wealth. The poor and the rich; the fast and the slow. Slow is a speed. Speed is a measure. I would even say that the speed of light—light-years, light-centuries—is nothing in the universe, since it dwells in the infinite. On the other hand, on Earth, speed abolishes, exterminates. Thereby the relation to profit is exterminated by the political economy of speed—instantaneity, ubiquity, immediacy. These three terms put an end to the economy.

Is instantaneity a form of deregulation in the field of vision as well?

The aesthetic problem is linked to the phenomenon of perception. This is why I am a phenomenologist. A dromologist[28] is a phenomenologist. Aesthetics was linked to the aesthetics of apparition in the visual field, either through perspective, or through the effects of successive horizons, from the clear to the vague, etc., all the way up to the negative horizon—a horizon in which there's only the horizon, and nothing else. One could say that the property of traditional painting was to allow the progressive emergence of a sketch, drawing, values. Finally one applied a varnish, and that was Leonardo Da Vinci, or Vermeer's *The Lacemaker*—the optical effect.

Deregulation began with the invention of cinematography—followed, of course, by television—with the aesthetics of disappearance.[29] Things exist all the more outwardly when they're animated and disappear, the preceding image yielding to the next one, in the videogram-photogram-frame sequence, etc. Images are all the more present when they escape, existing more through their disappearance than their appearance. Afterwards, we had cinemascope, the big screen, the *dissolving view,* and cutaway phenomena. The deregulation of perception was therefore carried out by way of the preeminence of the moving image, which has contaminated the fixed image. We can't really understand reality anymore without considering what I've called *dromoscopy*, the vision of speed, vision in movement, cinematics. When you look at a tree it moves a bit because of the wind, but it stands still. On the other hand, the tree that I see from the window of a TGV is another tree altogether, a tree in time, the time parading by, and this tree has meant more to the art of painting than the stationary tree painted by Nicholas Poussin. In the past, to be admitted to the Academy des Beaux

Arts, you were told to "paint a tree, whichever you'd like, the way you want it to be." It wasn't that stupid. They could see if the candidate was good at drawing and a good observer since the two went together. The tree was the entrance exam for an artist.

There is a relation between speed and light. The tree which he drew was the light of the tree.

In my opinion that's where deregulation started. It began with the moving image.

Before even it spread elsewhere?

Yes, in my opinion. Not only the industrial revolution, but all the revolutions began in the eighteenth century. And I really believe it was by way of machines. The first speed machines were vision machines. I believe that the vision machine was more important for modernity than transportation machines. When we're told that it was the locomotive, the steam machine which created the industrial revolution, I say no. It was the vision machine. First of all the telescope, since modernity, I'm sorry, was not the industrial revolution; rather it was astronomy, Copernicus, Galileo. Furthermore, in terms of history, modernity begins with them. For myself it began with machines of speed which are vision machines. The telescope is a *jet*, it propels perception. The telescope, by way of its telephoto lens, modified our relation to the world at the speed of light, before the speed of light of electromagnetic waves of the television existed.

Speed destroys real space in favor of real time, the time of globalization.

Globalization exists only in time. Real time dominates real space, the real space of continents, of miles, etc., everything that made for the grandeur of battlefields and fields of operation, for colonial forces as well as national forces. Everything that is now dominated by instantaneity, ubiquity, and immediacy, that is to say, everything that makes it possible for an important action occurring in a single place to have immediate consequences. This is valid on all levels, including for the stock market, which is in danger of crashing far more seriously than it did in 1929, since all the stock markets are now interconnected. Let's remember that instantaneity, ubiquity, and immediacy—*real time*—are the attributes of the divine. *Real space* was an attribute of the human being—whether king or emperor, still a human being. They didn't mistake themselves for God, even if occasionally they seemed to believe it; the tyrant like-wise. This is why I say: "What threatens democracy today is no particular tyrant, a Mao, a Hitler, it's tyranny when it takes up res-idence in immediacy, ubiquity, instantaneity." Technology appropriated divinity, so we don't need a person for that; anyone can avail themselves of this absolute power. Tyranny is already there, in microprocessor memory chips, and in immediacy and this "globalization of affects," as I call it, the fact that we can experience the same thing on the world scale. Total War was just tinkering compared to that.

The non-stop bombardment of information in real time has replaced the waves of planes that hit Nantes. We're all shuddering together, but we don't see the buildings fall. Affects come and go at full speed, replacing each other without leaving a trace behind. Interactivity keeps the world in a kind of tetanic trance, at once inert and overexcited, sleepwalking on a planetary scale.

This is a phenomenon of bewilderment, of conditioning. Before there was a society that standardized opinions, the press revolution of the nineteenth century: first of all product standardization, then the industrial revolution of standards. They reproduced the same, then used it to standardize opinions: Left, Right, Center. It still was representative democracy, but based on standardization, facilitated by the freedom of the press and then by the radio, etc. Now we are no longer in the era when opinions are standardized, but *emotions synchronized*. Past societies were based on force, or law or a community of reciprocal interests: the poor, the rich, etc. They called that community of interests, or social classes. Today we've become a community of emotions. The dictatorship of the proletariat was the Communism of social class. Now we entered into the Communism of affects. Affects can be effected instantly on the world scale. There is a sort of Communist Globalitarianism no longer based on interest (rich and poor, social justice) but on the fact of sharing emotions with millions, even billions of individuals. This Communism of affects is something unprecedented that no one has really noticed. Essentially we're dealing here with a religion. The synchronization of emotions is a phenomenon of a religious-mystical order. I say that as a Christian, and don't at all stop being Christian in saying it. The strength of a religious upbringing is that it allows one to understand what is religious in what is not, just as a convinced atheist can detect the atheism hiding in mysticism.

Is this Communism of affects at work in perception? Has there been a comparable impoverishment of vision?

As I see it, tele-objectivity is an infirmity. A modification in the field of perception has occurred, and we've lost lateralization. Now we're confined to frontal vision. You could think of it as a kind of glaucoma, which is a malady in optics. And what I say is that actually what brought about this mental pathology was instrumental pathology. The photograph represents a considerable reduction of the field of perception. We cannot understand contemporary art without taking into account the impact this arraignment of perception has had. In a sense the screen is a place where frontality is resolved, while laterality is more a part of vision itself. With vision the lateral is as important, if not more so, than frontal vision. This is as true for hunters as for animals. Why so? Because one needs to see something appear in one's field. One can cope with something coming right in front of you; but on the other hand if something, an animal or event comes at you sideways and you're not capable of perceiving it, then you're going to be had, caught by surprise. Therefore the field of laterality is very much part of attention, the optical field of attention, whereas the frontal is decision, acting out: "I'm taking aim." This is why our grandmothers used to tell us: "Don't point at someone with your finger. It's not polite." Because it's a threatening gesture. Confronting frontally, aiming, even with a finger, is a threat.

The sailor who was aiming at your childhood sweetheart on the terrace in Nantes had his finger on the trigger. Now you don't need a trigger anymore.

Yes, there is no more finger now; the target is the screen. You aim and at the same time are aimed at. The lateral is lost. Hence the question: "Where are you?" The cell phone is quite amazing about that. The GPS [Global Positioning System] involves a loss of lateral proximity, and even more so with multiple screens... When you're on the freeway and speeding at 150 mph, even faster—I did that in a friend's car—you're in the same logic of transmission; you're focused and your attention is targeted, and reduced. In the old days aiming was called perceptive faith. The line between the eyepiece and the notch was called *the line of faith*. Why? Because you only squeeze the trigger when you believe you'll hit the target. Nowadays they call it the "line of sight," which is stupid, since this is obviously what it is. The line of faith was so much more intelligent. The "line of sight" referred to a tool, so the proof of faith was in my squeezing the trigger at the moment I believed I would hit the target; but this was only a belief. Whereas perception machines are linked to faith in perception. Faith in perception is really a key notion, connoting religious faith. To believe in God is to believe what you see. Faith, belief, and vision are the basis for philosophical questions: since I saw it, I believe in it.

Do you really believe that there is a connection between faith and perception?

I believe that art and philosophy are the origins of the vision of the world. "Perceptive faith" is not something that I invented. The noun *faith* has disappeared, which is curious, since it is an absolute philosophical noun; which brings us back to the judgment made on Baudrillard: he didn't believe in tele-reality. This is the great question of perceptive faith: either I believe what I see, or I don't. This is the basis of faith, material as well as religious. Now listen to what Frederico Fellini said: "In essence, art is a call for mystery. Even beyond the religious expressions it may take, authentic art has a profound affinity with the world of faith." I believe that the grandeur of poverty takes us back to metaphysics. It will become necessary to return to metaphysical questions, even in politics. We're not going back to the wars of religion, but to philosophy.

And you, do you believe in tele-reality?

Of course not. I believe in God, therefore in Christ. I am a Christian.
You know, after the war the situation in France was clear-cut: either
you were a Communist or a Christian. There were these two alter-
natives, and no others. I converted when I paid a visit to pals
working in a factory. I couldn't enter a church, it horrified me. I just
couldn't do it. I came from a poor background, a Communist
family. One day I went to see a *curé* who lived in an attic, someone
remarkably intelligent, and we got along very well. I am a man of
religious faith and profoundly interested in perceptive faith. I am a
phenomenologist the way Edith Stein, Husserl's assistant, also was a
phenomenologist. She ended up in Auschwitz. She was a Carmelite,
she was Jewish and had converted. She tried to convert Husserl,
who was her boss. Husserl was close to converting, but finally said
to her: "No, I just can't abandon the world like that." So I am a
Husserlian. When I taught my first course at the College of Philosophy, everybody was talking about the Heidegger controversy at
the time: he was supposed to be a bad philosopher because he was
stained by Nazism, etc. So I told them what I thought: "Listen,
Caravaggio was a murderer, and this didn't prevent him from being
a great painter. You can be a great philosopher and a real bastard
too." A dromologist is naturally a phenomenologist since speed is a
relation *between* things. At the same time I am a converted Christian,
that is to say someone who doesn't believe in death, who believes in
a passage without concrete, without concrete corridors.

*So in your disagreement with Baudrillard, tele-reality wasn't really
the problem.*

No, actually we had a radically different approach to things. For me, things have a purpose, every moment has its purpose. He didn't believe so. This is why we could never discuss certain subjects. On the other hand, we had something in common, which was the uncertainty principle, not believing your own eyes, conscientious objections. This is why he wrote what he did about the Gulf War. There are conscientious objectors who don't want to see the war and those who don't believe in the war, even when it takes place, since the war was created out of its image: *Desert screen, desert storm.* These are major questions, and the curtain is about to rise.

Yes, if there is a curtain.

Finitude is the lifting of the curtain; no longer the horizon, but the horizon of a vertical littoral; until now our littoral was horizontal, conquerors and colonizers. Now we've entered into the vertical littoral. There is the Earth and Nothing, zero and the infinite.

In the "towerism" we talked about earlier, all we could see in the distance was vertical bunkers.

Yes, that was also an escape.

But not an escape into the future, a fall upwards.

Yes, a fall upwards.

— *Translated by Philip Beitchman*

Notes

Pure War

1. Paul Virilio, *Bunker Archéologie* (Paris: Centre Georges Pompidou, 1975).

2. Pierre Clastres, *Society Against the State* (New York: Urizen, 1977).

3. Paul Virilio, *L'insecurité du territoire* (Paris: Editions Stock, 1976).

4. Georges Duzémil, *Mythe et epopé* (Paris: Gallimard, 1968); *Idées romaines* (*ibid.*, 1969).

5. Jean Baudrillard, *In the Shadow of the Silent Majorities* and *Simulations* (New York: Semiotext(e) Foreign Agents Series, 1983).

6. Georges Duby, *Les Trois ordres de l'imaginaire du feodalisme* (Paris: Gallimard, 1978).

7. Paul Virilio, *The Aesthetics of Disappearance*, trans. Philip Beitchman, (New York: Semiotext(e) Double Agents Series, 1991).

8. Gilles Deleuze/Félix Guattari, *Mille Plateaux* (Paris: Minuit, 1980).

9. René Lorau, *L'auto-dissolution des avant-gardes* (Paris: Galiée, 1980).

10. Sylvère Lotringer and Christian Marazzi, *Autonomia: Post-Political Politics* (New York: Semiotext(e) Foreign Agents, 2007).

11. In "The German Issue," *Semiotext(e)* 11 (1982).

12. Luce Irigaray, *Speculum* (Paris: Minuit, 1974); *Ce sexe qui n'en est pas un* (ibid., 1977).

13. Jean Baudrillard, *Symbolic Exchange and Death* (Paris: Sage, London 1993).

14. Hélene Carrere, *Decline of an Empire: The Soviet Socialist Republics in Revolt* (New York: Newsweek Books, 1979).

15. In "The German Issue," *Semiotext(e)* 11 (1982).

POSTCRIPT 1997: INFOWAR

16. Paul Virilio, *Un paysage d'événements* (Paris: Galilée, 1996).

17. Paul Virilio, *The Vision Machine* (Bloomington: University of Indiana Press, 1994).

18. Paul Virilio, *The Art of the Motor* (Minneapolis: University of Minnesota Press, 1995).

19. Paul Virilio, *The Aesthetics of Disappearance*, trans. Philip Beitchman, (New York: Semiotext(e) Double Agents Series, 1991).

20. The Abbé Pierre is a popular figure in France through his work on behalf of the poor and homeless. More recently, he has lost some of his luster over his support of "revisionist" history.

21. Paul Virilio, *Speed and Politics* (New York: Semiotext(e) Foreign Agents Series, 1986).

POSTCRIPT 2007: WAR ON THE CITIES

22. Discussion in La Rochelle, France, June 19, 2007.

23. Bernard Kouchner is a French politician, diplomat, and doctor. He is co-founder of Doctors Without Borders (MSF).

24. Alain Krivine is a leader of the Trotskyist movement in France. He is a member of the Ligue Communiste Révolutionnaire (LCR).

25. Jean Duvignaud (1921–2007) was a writer, theater scholar and sociologist.

26. Jacques Rancière is a French philosopher and Professor of Philosophy at the University of Paris, author, among other books, of *Hatred of Democracy*.

27. Michel Rocard, former Prime Minister of France and leader of the Socialist Party, is a member of the European Parliament.

28. Dromologist, from *dromos*, racing. "Dromology" is the science of speed.

29. Paul Virilio, *The Aesthetic of Disappearance*, trans. Philip Beitchman, New York, Semiotext(e), 1991.

Index

and art of engine, 191; and
consciousness, 49. *See also*
Consciousness; Montage;
Picnolepsy

Cinematography, 228

Citizens: as passengers, 77–78

Citizenship, 125, 147, 149

City: anti-, 7, 9, 211; art of defending,
99; as battlefield, 9–11, 209, 218;
of dead time, 22; as dissolved by
speed, 73–75; and endo-colonization,
125; origins of, 19–20, 38; as
relation to politics, 17, 121; riddle
of, 77; universality of, 61

Civilians: war on, 210

Civilian soldiers, 34. *See also* Citizens;
Perversion

Clastres, Pierre, 19, 142, 237 n.2

Clausewitz, Carl von, 8, 18, 31, 39,
53, 61–62, 170

Clemenceau, Georges, 23

Coastal region: as interruption, 128

Cocteau, Jean, 142

Cohn-Bendit, Daniel, 139

Cold war: end of, 185–189

College of Philosophy, 234

Colonization, 81, 107, 157. *See also*
Decolonization; Endo-colonization

Columbia, 8

Columbus, Christopher, 223

Commerce: and war, 20–21

Communication: weaponry of, 196–198

Communism, 61, 94, 142, 169,
171–172, 231, 234

Complete release, 62–64, 68

Computer, 113, 179; revolution,
188, 198

Conscientious objector, 235

Consciousness, 34, 47–50, 88–89, 93,
98, 133–134, 137, 139, 150. *See
also* Duration; Picnolepsy

Consumer society: movements against,
165, 215

Consumption: as definition or
destruction of society, 165. *See
also* Pure war

Copernicus, 224, 229

Cops, 121, 124

Corporations. *See* Multinationals

Corsica, 74

Coupling, 170. *See also* Fatal couple

Crusades, 64, 69

Daboville, 186

Dallas-Fort Worth, 77

Dardanelles, the, 173

Darfur, 210

DaVinci, Leonardo, 120, 228

Death, 17, 22, 47–48, 50–52, 62–63,
94, 120, 122, 133–143, 149-150,
163, 176, 180, 187–188, 212 213,
217, 234

Death penalty. *See* Capital punishment

Decline of an Empire. See Encausse,
Hélene Carrere d'

Decolonization: as sign of
endo-colonization, 166. *See also*
Colonization; Endo-colonization

Delacroix, Eugène, 120

Deleuze, Gilles, 53, 151, 201, 205;
(and Félix Guattari) *Milles
Plateaux*, 53, 237 n.8

Democracy, 9, 42, 111, 159, 201, 214,
216, 222–224, 230–231

Deterrence, 7, 9, 32, 39–40, 61, 67–71, 103–104, 106, 112, 117, 124, 130–132, 135, 146, 148–150, 156, 158, 161, 174, 177, 195–196, 198–200, 221; end of, 186–189; and technoscience, 187

Deterritorialization, 87, 121, 151–152, 158, 175

Dick, Philip K. (*Time Out of Joint*), 219

Dromocracy, 59, 71, 134

Dromology, 55, 95, 205, 228, 234, 239 n.28

Dromoscopy, 97, 228

Duby, Georges, 28, 237 n.6

Dumézil, Georges, 27–28, 237 n.4

Duration, 42, 48-49, 51, 60, 73, 86, 94, 110, 149–150

Duvignaud, Jean, 215, 239 n.25

École des Annales, 186

Ecologistics, 104

Ecology, 211, 224, 226

Egypt, 173

Eiffel Tower, 11

Einstein, Albert, 198

Eisenhower, 29–30, 32, 39, 105

El Salvador, 108–109

Emotion(s), 69, 96, 213; synchro- nization of, 214, 231. *See also* Affects

Encausse, Hélene Carrere d' (*Decline of an Empire*), 164, 238 n.14

Endo-colonization: continual intensification of, 185; as destruc- tion of society, 68; and intensive- ness, 107; as model of political State, 166; and opposition to war- machine, 132; as population control, 125; as predictable tendency, 159; as exterminating opposition, 178; and societal non development, 164; and State-as- destiny, 109-111. *See also* Colonization; Decolonization

Enemy, the, 11, 33, 104, 107, 115, 119, 163,193–194, 196, 210; civilians as, 210; as a terrorist, 193; as our own weaponry and intelligence, 35, 61

Energy crisis, 78

England, 29, 73, 110, 156, 158, 172

Engels, Friedrich, 117

Enlightenment, Age of, 76

Entebbe, 41

Epilepsy, 48

Escape velocity, 201–202

Esso, 35

Esthétique de la disparition, L'. See Virilio, Paul—*Aesthetics of Disappearance*

Euclid, 93, 226

Europe: analysis of history of, 28; and autonomy, 111; and colonization, 109, 157; effect of north-south axis on, 174; effect of speed on, 173; elimination and Third World-ization of, 156–157; and genetically engineered products, 188; and pacifism, 131, 161; and recognition of defeat, 171; societal nondevelopment of, 105–106; time in, 205; and Total War, 18, 23–24; and US military opposition, 178; and Welfare State, 109

Evolution, 60, 166; -ism, 46
Extreme sports, 187–188

Falklands war, 33, 35, 40, 61, 156,
    173–174
Fascism, 37, 203
Fascists: and science, 188
Fatal couple, 129–130, 169. *See also*
    Coupling
FBI, 204
Feedback, 201
Fellini, Frederico, 233
Ferry, Abel, 31
Finitude, 222–226, 235
Fondation Cartier, 213
Food, 31. *See also* Genetically
    engineered products
Foucault, Michel, 52, 69
Fractal(s), 49, 124
France: and death penalty, 135; effect
    of speed on, 73; availability of
    information in, 146; interpretations
    of Virilio in, 91–92; military
    research in, 72; and naval power,
    158; politics and military in,
    22–23; and recognition of defeat,
    171; Revolution of (1789), 70;
    role of police in, 107; Terror in,
    116; and use of technology, 92
Franco-Prussian war, 118
Freedom, 76, 83–84, 113; and
    oil flows, 175
"Free radio," 92–94
Freud, Sigmund, 137, 140, 219
Friedman, Milton, 110
Fukuyama, Francis, 205
Fuller, General, 71, 83

Futurism, 37, 54

Galileo, 224, 229
Galtieri, General, 40–41
Gaza, 210
Genetics, 188
Genetically engineered products, 188.
    See also Food
Genghis Khan, 222
Geopolitics, 7, 10–11, 21, 51, 121,
    127, 131, 140, 147. *See also*
    Chronopolitics; Metropolitics;
    Politics; Transpolitics
Geostrategy, 21, 158, 177; and domestic
    exploitation, 177; notion of,
    outmoded by sophisticated
    weapons, 131; organization of,
    173; and space-time, 175. *See
    also* Space-time
Geostrategic delirium, 8
Gericault, Théodore, 120
Germany, 24, 101, 131, 147, 151
Gibraltar, 173–174
Glemp, Józef, 160, 162
Globalitarianism, 11–12, 231
Globalization, 7–8, 201–203, 209,
    222–223, 227, 229–230
God, 51, 132–133, 140–143, 176,
    196–197, 203, 215, 230, 233–
    234; death of, 141–142
Goebbels, Joseph, 196
GPS, 232
Greece, 77
Grimaud, Pierre, 215
Gromyko, Andrei, 42–43
Guantanamo, 9
Guatamala, 108, 188

Guevara, Che, 215
Gulag, 146–147
Gulf war, 186, 191, 235

Haiti, 188
Hamlet, 205
Hautes Études de Défense Nationale,
    Institut des, 22
Heidegger, Martin, 37, 133, 234
Heisenberg, Werner, 11
Hezbollah, 10–11, 210
Hirohito, 213
Hiroshima, 9, 71, 106, 190, 212
History: disappearance/end of, 52,
    186, 205, 223
Hitler, 213, 222, 230
Hölderlin, Friedrich, 119
Holy War, 63-64, 67, 141, 146, 160,
    163, 176
Hong Kong, 112, 179
Hughes, Howard, 84, 86–88; *Ice
    Station Zebra*, 87
Hugo, Victor, 97
Hunthausen, Raymond G. (Archbishop
    of Seattle), 145–146
Huns, 177
Husserl, Edmund, 234

Ice Station Zebra. See Hughes, Howard
Ideology, 17, 34, 63, 69, 82, 108, 129,
    147, 149, 152, 172, 222
Illich, Ivan, 36
Indian Ocean, 131, 174
Industrial Revolution, 59, 166, 222,
    229, 231
Information: bomb, 198–199, 201, 230;
    and deterrence, 195, 199–200; as

interactivity, 198, 200; and
    resistance to Pure War, 146;
    technology, 196, 224
Infowar, 192, 194–195, 198, 204
Insécurité du territoire, L'. See Virilio, Paul
Instantaneousness, 42–43, 60, 72–73,
    75, 79, 101, 132, 167
Intensity, 110, 150, 152
Interactivity, 198, 200–201, 230
Inter-American Treaty on Reciprocal
    Assistance, 107
Internet, 199, 201
Iran, 11, 13, 39–40, 63, 160, 193
Iraq, 10, 39, 63, 191, 195
Iraqi war, so-called. *See* Gulf war
Irigaray, Luce, 124, 237 n.12
Islam, 63–64, 133, 160, 164, 210
Israel, 40–41, 63, 133, 153, 188, 210.
    See also Arab-Israeli conflict

Japan, 199; suicide project of, 212–213;
    Aum Shinrykio gassing in, 189
Japanese Red Army, 213
Jaruzelski, Wojciech, 159–160, 162
Jerusalem, 78, 133
Jesuits, 24, 125
Jomini, Henri, 31
Jünger, Ernst (*The Universal State*),
    112, 218

Kamikaze: as opposite of politics, 179
Kania, Stanislaw, 159, 162
Kennedy, John F., 71
Kerouac, Jack, 54
Khomeini, Ayatollah, 40, 64, 160
Kipling, Rudyard, 96, 102
Klein, Hans-Joachim, 123

Knowledge, 69; perversion of field of, 36; delirium of, 188; humility as precondition of, 225

Kouchner, Bernard, 209–210, 238 n.23

Kraus, Chris, 204

Khrushchev, Nikita, 71, 105, 165

Krivine, Alain, 215, 239 n.24

Kübler-Ross, Elisabeth, 137

Landscape of Events, A. *See* Virilio, Paul

Lasers, 69, 72, 130–131

Las Vegas, 87

Latin America. *See* South America

Law, 135–137

Lebanon, 10, 63, 136, 160, 210

Lenin, Vladimir I., 155

Liberation, 122, 124, 188; speed, 201–202; women's, 122–124

Libération, 202

Libya, 193

Light-speed, 201

Lima, 189

Lindberg, Charles, 86

Liverpool, 73

Lockheed, 86

Logistics, 20, 30–32, 83, 103–104, 153, 166, 196, 221

London, 9, 11, 22, 73, 209

Lourau, René (*L'Auto-dissolution des avant-gardes*), 95, 237 n.9

Los Angeles, 21; riots, 197

Louis XVI, 139

Lyon, 73

Lyotard, Jean-François, 49

Maginot Line, 10, 18, 127

Malinovsky, Rodin, 105

Malraux, André, 153

Mandelbrot, Benoît, 49

Maoism, 172

Marinetti, Felippo T., 54

Mao, 230

Martian Chronicles, The. See Bradbury, Ray

Marx, Karl, 45, 73, 94, 106, 117–118, 134, 172, 224

Marxism, 116–118, 124, 153; and ideology, 172

Mauritius, 158

May '68, 94, 165, 197, 215

McLuhan, Marshall, 54

McNamara, Robert, 42–43

Media: explosion, 194–195; and terrorism. *See* Terrorism—and mass communication

Menander, 133

Metabolic speed, 43–44, 150

Metropoli, 92

Metropolitics, 7, 11, 209. *See also* Chronopolitics; Geopolitics; Politics; Transpolitics

Meza, General, 107

Middle East, 10, 64, 131

Miletus, 77, 115

Military: the a-national, 30, 32, 106; architecture, 18; -industrial complex, 24, 71, 105, 112, 170, 187, 191; budget of, 70, 109, 131, 185, 193; space, 18; thought, 170; as triumph of logistics, 32

Milles Plateaux. See Deleuze, Gilles

Mobile phone. *See* Telephone—portable

Mogadishu, 41

Montage, 48–49. *See also* Cinema;
    Consciousness; Picnolepsy
Morand, Paul, 53
Moscow, 78, 99, 130
Movement, 78, 84, 88
Müller, Heiner, 164
Multimedia explosion, 195
Multinationals, 34, 39, 59, 111–113
Music, 192
Myth, 18–19, 22, 27-29, 50, 62, 85,
    115, 136, 142, 160, 177

NAFTA, 13
Nagasaki, 9, 212
Nantes, 18, 218–220, 230, 232
Napoléan, 24, 45, 58, 196
Napoleanic wars, 31
NASA, 226
Nation-State. *See* State-Nation
National Academy of Sciences, 189
National security, 107, 116; Agency
    (NSA), 190, 204
NATO, 61, 163
Nature, 36, 43, 64, 226
Nazi culture, 213
Nazi Germany, 101, 147
Neolithic Age, 19, 151
Nepal, 74
New York, 9, 11, 21, 74, 78, 82, 86,
    209, 217
New Yorker, The, 125
Nicaragua, 124
Nietzsche, Friedrich, 52, 141–142, 214
Nineteenth century, 24, 47, 58, 85–86,
    99, 151
Nixon, Richard, 130, 170–171
Nomadism, 77, 84, 88, 102, 152

Northern Ireland, 190
North-South conflict, 68
Nuclear: accident, 198; age, 71, 133,
    151; anti-, 139; death, 50–51, 62,
    143, 164; faith, 61, 68–69, 132;
    power, 60–61, 64, 74, 111, 146,
    153, 158, 170, 181, 189, 199;
    proliferation, 7–8, 69, 188–189,
    200; revolution, 171; suicide, 164;
    threat, 67, 126, 194, 209; warfare,
    32, 35, 40, 43, 64, 76, 117, 125,
    128, 130–131, 145, 181, 196,
    209, 221; weapon(s), 11, 31, 42,
    70, 72, 105, 152, 174, 179–180,
    190, 200

Odeon theatre, 94, 215–216
Oil, 35, 156, 174–175
Oklahoma City bombings, 189–190
Olympic Games, 99
Ordre Nouveau, 121
Orly, 79
Orpheus, 142

Pace, Lanfranco, 92
Pacifists, 132, 148, 161–163
Palestine, 210
Paris, 11–12, 21, 74–75, 78, 82, 118,
    205, 213, 215, 218; Commune,
    12, 118, 172
Patriot Act, The, 9
Peace. *See* Pacifists; Peace movement;
    Total peace
Peace movement, 131, 133, 145–151
    passim, 160
Pentagon, 12, 32, 170, 194, 198,
    204–205

Schopenhauer, Arthur, 97
Science: as race to death, 188; as fascist
science, 188; as Pure War, 187,
191, 205; humility as foundation
of, 225. *See also* Technoscience
SEATO, 61
Seattle, 145
Sedentariness, 19–21, 75, 77–79, 86,
88, 94, 152
September 11, 215, 217
Sevestre, Admiral, 117
Seychelles, the, 158
Shanghai, 211
Sharon, General, 63
Siegfried Line, 18, 127
Situationism, 215
Six Days war, 10, 39
Smith, Adam, 73
Socialism, 118, 172
Sociology, 17, 25, 27, 29
Somalia, 194
Sorbonne, 94, 216
South Africa, 174, 188
South America, 8; colonization and
underdevelopment of, 109; and
dictatorship of movement, 78;
and deterritorialization, 175;
effect of north-south axis on, 174;
as laboratory of future society,
107–108, 165; as laboratory for
politics of disappearance, 100–101;
nondevelopment of, 173; and US
military opposition, 178
Soutine, Chaim, 120
Soviet Union. *See* USSR
Space-time: and field of shrinking
freedom, 83; of speed and

communications, 99; struggle to
produce a, 175. *See also*
Chronopolitics; Geostrategy
Spain, 101
Spanish Civil War, 12
Speed, 17, 21, 22, 35, 43-49 *passim*,
57–59, 69, 75–89 *passim*, 96–99,
132–134, 150, 188, 192, 194,
201–202, 205, 222, 226–230,
232, 234; absolute destruction of,
72, 74; and the city, 73, 77–78;
and computing, 205; as essence of
war, 166; as extermination of space,
87, 229; politicization of, 43; the
question of, 45, 71, 166; and space
of freedom, 83; as historic limit,
205; technology as producer of,
166. *See also* Metabolic speed
Speed and Politics. See Virilio, Paul
Speer, Albert, 29, 217
Sports. *See* Extreme sports
Stalin, Joseph, 169
Stampa, La, 158
Star Wars, 171
START agreements, 42, 130, 174
State, the: and absolute destruction, 60;
as constitutionally organized
technology of economic capitalization, 19; of emergency, 52,
59-60, 110, 124; and end of
politics, 152; history of, 211;
Nation-, 13, 21, 39, 59, 61, 103,
211; Pure, 50, 65, 111–112, 152,
175, 177; and relation to death,
120, 135; and societal nondevelopment, 111; suicide-, 102,
116, 163, 178-180; and terrorism,

39-41, 50, 61, 101–102, 113; violence vs., 65; and war, 118; Welfare, 109–110, 185

Stein, Edith, 234

Stock market crash (1929), 34, 230. *See also* Wall Street crash

Strike, the: 49, 53, 121, 123; as weapon, 160–161. *See also* Trade unionism

Subliminal advertising. *See* Advertising

Suez, 173–174

Suicide: mass, 213; national, individual, special right to commit, 163; as a weapon, 212. *See also* State—Suicide

Suicidal soldier, 212

Sun Tzu (*Art of War*), 53, 133

Surrealism, 215

Switzerland, 175

Syria, 193

Taxes, 57–59, 121, 146

Taylor, Maxwell, 105

Techné, 192

Technical horizon, 147, 152

Technology, 24, 29, 68, 121; riddle of, 36, 43, 45, 77, 93; war as source of, 38; and unbridled military intelligence, 35; as source of speed, 166; and art, 191–192; defective, 202; question of, 37

Technoscience, 187–188, 192

Tele-conferences, 75

Telegraph, 31, 58, 196

Telephone, 41, 74, 150; portable, 212, 232

Tele-reality, 224, 233–235

Telescope, 229

Television, 81, 88, 92, 96–97, 99–100, 192, 197, 228–229

Tendency, 27–30, 38, 53, 61–62, 75, 79, 87, 104, 112, 119, 148, 153, 156, 166, 177

Terrorism, 7–13, 34, 37, 39–41, 50, 61, 92, 101–102, 113, 122–123, 141, 161, 188-190, 193–194, 211–214; countries that support, 193; hyper-, 7, 9; and mass communication, 194

TGV. *See* Très Grande Vitesse

Third World, 85, 105–107, 116, 119, 157; within USA and USSR, 164

Three Mile Island, 198

Time, 74–75, 205; extensive vs. intensive, 110

Titanic, 199

Tofler, Alvin (*The Third Wave*), 126

Total peace, 104; as refusal to develop, 165; as war pursued by other means, 39

Total War, 7, 11–12, 18–19, 23–24, 32, 39, 50, 76, 164, 209, 214, 230

Towers, 11, 12, 87, 112, 126, 159, 190, 211, 216–217, 235

Toynbee, Philip, 19

Trade unionism, 118, 155, 159; as combat commando against management, 160; transformation of, 162

Trans-political war, 7-8

Transpolitics, 8, 13, 42, 105, 110, 132, 136, 148, 153, 224. *See also* Chronopolitics; Geopolitics; Metropolitics; Politics

Transportation Revolution. *See* Industrial Revolution

Très Grande Vitesse (TGV), 126, 226, 228

Trotsky, Leon, 118

Twin Towers. *See* World Trade Center

Ultimate weapon. *See* Nuclear-weapon

Uncertainty principle, 10, 11, 235

Unknown quantity, 148

Urbanization, 100, 112, 125, 211

Uruguay, 109

USA, 29, 72–73, 85, 105–106, 109–110, 113, 118, 156; and coupling, 130, 170; dependence of USSR on, 166; effect of north-south axis on, 174; as empire, 172; and end of cold war, 189; and endo-colonization at its best, 185; first military defeat of, 171; and ideological conflict, 176; as threatened by its own supremacy, 194

USSR: collapse of, 185–186; and coupling, 170; effect of north-south axis on, 174; as empire, 172; and end of cold war, 189; and fatal coupling, 130; and ideological conflict, 176; and information scarcity, 169; military research in, 72; nondevelopment of, 166, 173; and north-south inversion, 156–157, 164; and political-military tension, 171; and social promotion via military development, 108–109; and strategic consumption, 105

Valéry, Paul, 222

Vatican II: and deterrence, 161

Vauban, 153, 218

Verdun, 10, 12, 180, 212

Vermeer (*The Lacemaker*), 228

Verne, Jules, 46, 81

Vietnam, 106, 130, 152, 156–157, 170, 172; war, 130, 152

Villette, La, 47

Virilio, Paul: as a Christian, 63, 118, 132, 141, 231, 234; writing style of, 52; *Aesthetics of Disappearance*, 47, 53–54, 134, 150, 191, 228, 237 n.7, 238 n.19; *The Art of the Motor*, 191, 238 n.18; *Bunker Archeology*, 19, 220, 237 n.1; *Ground Zero*, 213; *L'insécurité du territoire*, 21, 38, 130, 151, 164, 220, 237 n.7; *A Landscape of Events*, 186–187, 238 n.16; *Open Sky*, 201–202; *Popular Defense and Ecological Struggles*, 92, 95, 152; *Pure War*, 7, 185, 187, 221; *Speed and Politics*, 53–55, 91, 95, 98–99, 201, 238 n.21; *La stratégie de l'au-dela*, 54; *The Vision Machine*, 191, 238 n.17; *War and Cinema*, 96

Virtual reality, 191

Vision, 48, 96, 228–229, 232–233

Vision Machine, The. See Virilio, Paul

Vitesse de libération, La. See Virilio, Paul—*Open Sky*

Walesa, Lech, 160–164

Wall Street crash (1987), 200. *See also* Stock market crash

War: automation of, 85; becomes State terrorism, 40; on civilians, 210; as classically understood, 39; as death of city, 22; ideological, 172, 176; as logistics, 166; opposition to, 33; of tribes vs. State, 19. *See also* Algerian war; Cold war; Commerce—and war; Endo-colonization—and opposition to war-machine; Europe—and Total War; Falklands war; Franco-Prussian war; Gulf war; Holy War; Infowar; Napoleonic wars; Nuclear—warfare; Pure war; Science-as Pure War; Six Days war; Spanish Civil War; Speed—as essence of war; Star wars; State, the—and war; Technology—war as source of; Total peace—as war pursued by other means; Total War; Transpolitical war; USA—and end of cold war; USSR—and end of cold war; Vietnam—war; War-machine; World War I; World War II

War-machine, 22, 33, 35, 38, 58, 64, 68, 93, 102, 118–119, 122, 130–132, 145–147, 171, 173, 179–180, 201; and elimination of individuals, 179; as societal non-development, 176

Warsaw Pact, 65, 155, 159, 163

Watergate, 170-171

Weaponry: three ages of military, 195; as enemy. See Enemy. *See also* Communication; Weapons proliferation

Weapons proliferation, 190. *See also* Nuclear—proliferation

Welfare State. *See* State—Welfare

Welles, Orson (*War of the Worlds*), 198

White House, 105

Women's liberation, 122, 124

World Bank, 112

World Cup, 100

World Trade Center (WTC), 12, 185–186, 189–190, 194–195, 210, 216–217

World War I, 23-24, 29, 31, 180

World War II, 9, 18, 21, 29, 39, 101, 203

Yalta Agreements, 61, 157

Yugoslavia, ex-, 186, 193

Zhukov, Georgy, 105

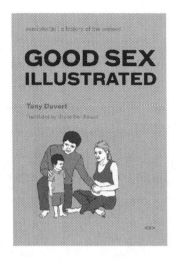

GOOD SEX ILLUSTRATED
Tony Duvert, translated by Bruce Benderson

Written in the wake of May 1968 and Deleuze and Guattari's *Anti-Oedipus*, Tony Duvert's *Good Sex Illustrated* (*Le bon sexe illustré*) was part of the miraculous moment when sexuality could turn the world upside down and reveal social hypocrisy for what it was. Bitterly funny and unabashedly anarchistic, *Good Sex Illustrated* openly declares war on mothers, family, psychoanalysis, morality, and the entire social construct, through a close reading of sex manuals for children. Published in 1973, one year after Duvert won the prestigious Prix Médicis, it proved that accolades had not tempered his scathing wit or his approach to such taboo topics as pedophilia. This translation, by award-winning author Bruce Benderson, will belatedly introduce English-speaking audiences to the most infamous gay writer from France since Jean Gênet first hit the scene in the '40s.
6 x 9 • 184 pages • ISBN-13: 978-1-58435-043-9 • $14.95

OVEREXPOSED
Sylvère Lotringer
With a new introduction by the author and an additional chapter.

The most perverse perversions are not always those one would expect. Originally conceived as an American update to Foucault's *History of Sexuality*, *Overexposed* is even more outrageous and thought-provoking today than it was twenty years ago when it was first published. Half-way between *Dr. Strangelove* and *Clockwork Orange*, this insider's exposition of cutting-edge cognitive behavioral methods is a hallucinating document on the limits presently assigned to humanity. It also offers a reflection on the overall 'obscenity' of contemporary society where everything, and not just sex, is exposed in broad daylight to quickly sink into complete indifference.

"*Overexposed* is an engrossing description of sexual conditioning condoned by the state. A fascinating book."
— William Burroughs
6 x 9 • 192 pages • ISBN-13: 978-1-58435-045-3 • $14.95

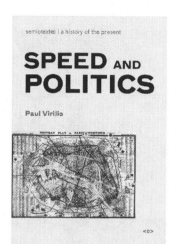

SPEED AND POLITICS
Paul Virilio, translated by Mark Polizzotti
Introduction by Benjamin Bratton

Speed and Politics (1986; first published in France in 1977) is the matrix of Virilio's entire work. Building on the works of Morand, Marinetti, and McLuhan, Virilio presents a vision more radically political than that of any of his French contemporaries: speed as the engine of destruction. It presents a topological account of the entire history of humanity, honing in on the technological advances made possible through the militarization of society. Written at a lightning-fast pace, Virilio's landmark book is an split-second, overwhelming look at how humanity's motivity has shaped the way we function today, as well as a view into what might come of it.

6 x 9 • 176 pages • ISBN-13: 978-1-58435-040-8 • $14.95

FORGET FOUCAULT
Jean Baudrillard, Introduction by Sylvère Lotringer

In 1976, Jean Baudrillard sent this essay to the French magazine *Critique*, of which Michel Foucault was an editor. Foucault was asked to reply, but remained silent. *Oublier Foucault* (1977) made Baudrillard instantly infamous in France. It was a devastating revisitation of Foucault's recent *History of Sexuality* and of his entire œuvre. Also an attack on those philosophers, like Gilles Deleuze and Felix Guattari, who believed that 'desire' could be revolutionary. In Baudrillard's eyes, desire and power were exchangeable, so desire had no place in Foucault. There is no better introduction to Baudrillard's polemical approach to culture than these pages where he dares Foucault to meet the challenge of his own thought. First published in 1987 in America with a dialogue with Sylvère Lotringer : *Forget Baudrillard*, this new edition contains a new introduction by Lotringer revisiting the ideas and impact of this singular book.

6 x 9 • 144 pages • ISBN-13: 978-1-58435-041-5 • $14.95

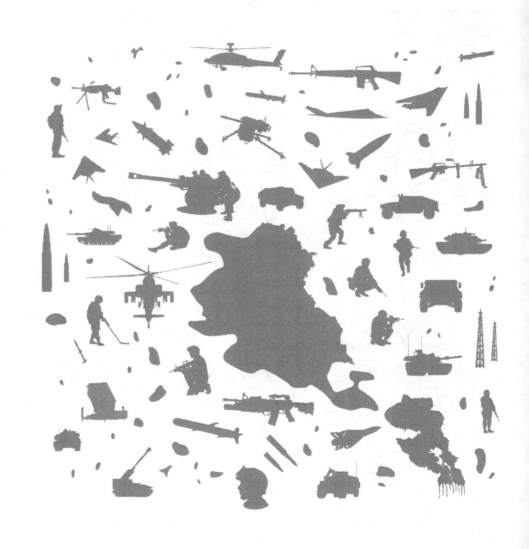

Printed in the United States
by Baker & Taylor Publisher Services